FORGOTTEN HOUSES OF HOLYWOOD

Author & Publisher
Con Auld
2003
Holywood, County Down
Northern Ireland

First Published March, 2003
Published by Con Auld
"Martello Corner"
14 Victoria Road, Holywood
Co. Down, N.I. BT18 9BD
© Con Auld 2002

Printed by Spectator & Chronicle Newspaper Group
Balloo Industrial Estate Bangor N.I. BT19 7HJ

ISBN No. 0.9542274-1-7

All Rights Reserved. No part of this publication may be reproduced, stored in a retrieval system or transmitted in any form or any means, electronic, mechanical, photocopying, recording or otherwise without prior permission of the Author and Publisher in writing.
It will not be lent, resold or otherwise disposed of by way of trade in any form of binding or cover other than that in which it is published.

CONTENTS

INTRODUCTION   9

1. Abingdon, 48 Demesne Road, BT18 9EX (Now Demesne Close)   10
   (1) Abingdon, (c.1899) (2) St. Valentines (1897)

II. Agricultural College, 93/95 Victoria Road, BT18 9BG   12
    (3) The College (1849) (4) Burnleigh and Crofton (1850's)

III. Alma Terrace, 23/25 Church View (now Harbinson Mews) BT18 9OP   14
     (5) The Terrace (1858)

IV. Alms Houses, 108/114 Downshire Road, BT18 9LZ   15
    (6) The Alms Houses (1913)

V. Altona, 69, Church Road, BT18 9BX (now Altona Manor)   16
   (7) Altona (c. 1895).

VI. Ardtullagh (c. 1850) Redburn Country Park, BT18 9QH   17
    (8) Ardtullagh (9) Holywood Hill House (c.1850)
    (10) Old Golf Club (11) Keepers Cottage (c. 1850)

VII. Ardville, Old Quay Road and Pavillion
     Farmhill Road BT18 0AL   19
     (12) Ardville (c. 1850)

VIII. Ashfield, Belfast Road BT18 9QY
      (now Palace Military Barracks)   21
      (13) The Bishop's Palace (1827)

IX. Bath Cottage, Strand Avenue, BT19 9AN
    (now Holywood Throughpass)   23
    (14) The Cottage (c. 1850) (15) Old Presbyterian Kirk (c. 1750)
    (16) Stewart's Place Cottage (c.1865)

X. Ballymenoch House, Bangor Road, BT18 0LQ
   (now Salvation Army Residential Home)   25
   (17) The House (c. 1825) (18) Garden Façade (1912)
   (19) Holywood Gate Lodge (1805) (20) Bangor Gate Lodge (1805)
   (21) Estate Cottages at Bangor Gate (1830's)

CONTENTS

XI	Brooklyn 69 to 75 Victoria Road BT18 9BG (22) The House (c. 1850)	27
XII	Clanbrassil Terrace 2-6 Clanbrassil Road BT18 OAP (23) Artist's Impression of Completed Terrace (c. 1867)	29
XIII	Clanbrassil Villas 15 Seafront Road BT18 OBB (24) The Villas (c. 1866) (now Clanbrassil Court)	30
XIV	Craigavad House, Station Road Craigavad BT18 OBP (Now the Royal Belfast Golf Club) (25) The House (1847) (26) Belfast Road Gate Lodge (1850)	31
XV	Craigdarragh, Craigdarragh Road BT19 1UB (now St. Columbanus House) (27) The House (c. 1850) (28) Gate Lodge (1870)	33
XVI	Craigtara 1 My Lady's Mile BT18 9EW (29) The House (1896)	34
XVII	Croft Cottage, 2 Croft Road BT18 OPB (now Croft Rise) (30) The Cottage or The Croft (1868)	35
XVIII	Croft House, Croft Road BT18 OPB (Now Croft Manor) (31) Croft House (1866) (32) Woodburn House (1860's)	36
IXX	Crofton Hall, Bangor Road BT18 0NE (Now Crofton Glen) (33) The House (1867) (34) Gate Lodge (1867)	38
XX	Culloden, 140 Bangor Road BT18 OEY (Now Culloden Hotel) (35) The House (1876) (36) Gate Lodge (1876)	39
XXI	Cultra House, Cultra Avenue BT18 OCT (now Cultra Park) (37) Cultra House (1810's) (38) (Cultra Manor (1900's)	41
XXII	Dalcoolin, Bangor Road BT18 OEY (Now Ulster Transport Museum) (39) The House (c. 1867) (40) Entrance Front (c. 1867) (41) Gate Lodge (1860's)	43

CONTENTS

XXIII Easdale, 28 Victoria Road BT18 9BD   45
    (now Easdale Housing Development)
        (42) The House (c. 1860)

XXIV Elton House, The Kinnegar BT18 9JR   46
    (Now Army Property)
        (43) The House (c.1860) (44) Golf House (c. 1868)

XXV Esplanade Cottage, 1 The Esplande BT18 9JG   47
    (now semi-detached houses) (45) The Cottage (c. 1850)

XXVI Glencraig, Seahill Road BT18 0DA   48
    (Now Camphill Community)
        (46) Glencraig House (1833) (47) Craigowen (1860's)
        (48) Gate Lodge (1851)

XXVII Gray's Buildings, Marine Parade BT18 9HZ   50
    (Now South Entry to Throughpass Subway)
        (49) The Terrace (1830's)

XXVIII Hillbrook, 22 and 24 Victoria Road BT18 9BG (Extant)   51
        (50) The House (1852)

XXIX Holywood House, Abbey Place BT18 9PP   52
    (Now Loughview Housing Estate and S.U.S. Campus)
    (51) The House (1706) (52) The Courtyard (1706)
    (53) Gate Lodge (1860's)

XXX House of Industry, Marine Parade BT18 9HZ   54
    (now South entry to Throughpass Subway)
        (54) The House of Industry (c. 1813)

XXXI Killops Court, The High Street BT18 9AG   56
    (Now commercial development)
        (55) The Court (1840) (56) Numbers 66 to 72 High Street (1850)

CONTENTS

4XXXII to XXXIV Knocknagoney Trilogy   Belfast Road BT18 9QY   57
    (now Esporta and Police Service)
    (57) Knocknagoney House (1880) (58) Gate Lodge (c. 1820)
    (59)   Clifton (c. 1760) (60) Gardener's Lodge (1850's)
    (61) Farm Yard (1850's) (62) Estate Cottages (1850's)
    (63)   Mertoun Hall (c. 1820) (64) Gate Lodge (1850's)

XXXV   Lorne, Station Road BT18 0BP   61
    (Now Guide Association Headquarters)
    (65) The House (1873)

XXXVI to XXXIX   A Foursome of Manses   62
    (66)   Glenside, 79 Victoria Road BT18 9BG (c. 1850) (Extant)
    (67)   Beechcroft, 18 Croft Road BT18 0PB (1864)(Croft Meadows)
    (68)   Glenavon, 25 Church Avenue BT18 9BJ (1860's) (Extant)
    (69)   Church Hill, Church View (1864) (Demolished)

XL   Marine Cottage, Marine Parade BT18 9HY   64
    (Now Holywood Throughpass)
    (70)   The Cottage (c. 1820)

XLI   Marine Hotel, Marine Parade BT18 9HY   65
    (Now Holywood Throughpass)
    (71)   The Hotel (c. 1840)

XLII   Marmion Lodge, Church Road BT18 9BZ   66
    (Now Marmion Adolescent Unit)
    (72)   Marmion Lodge (1858)

XLIII Maryfield, 109 Belfast Road BT18 9QY   68
    (Now Northern Ireland Office)
    (73)   The House (c. 1830) (74) Gatelodge (c.1830).

XLIV Number 28, High Street BT18 9AD   69
    (Health Office and Priory Surgery)
    (75) The House (1850).

CONTENTS

XLV Oakley,   50 Belfast Road BT18 9EL   70
    (now Officers' Quarters Palace Military Barracks)
    (76) The House (1858)

XLVI O'Neill's Place, 21 Church Road BT18 9BU   72
    (Now O'Neill's Place Apartment Buildings)
    (77) The Court (c. 1840).

XLVII Patton's Lane, High Street and Church View (Extant) BT18 9DB   73
    (78)   Patton's Lane (c. 1840). (79) Old Palace Bar (c.1850)

XLVIII Pebble Lodge, Belfast Road BT18 9ES   74
    (Now The Parks Apartment Building)
    (80) The Lodge (c. 1870).

XLIX Redburn, Old Holywood Road BT18 9HQ   76
    (Now Holywood Nursing Home and Redburn Country Park)
    (81) The House (1866)   (82) Garden Façade (1866)
    (83) Front Porch (1866)   (84) Holywood Gate Lodge (1866)
    (85) Belfast Gate Cottages (1866)

L Redburn Square Number 7, BT18 9HZ   79
    (85)   House and Garden (1874)

LI Richmond Lodge Belfast Road BT4 2QQ   80
    (now Knocknagoney Housing Estate)
    (86) The Lodge (c. 1800) (87) Gate Lodge (c. 1875)

LII Riverston House, 66 Church Road BT18 9BU   82
    (now Nursery School and Telephone Exchange)
    (88)   The House (1858) (89) Brook Street Cottages (1780)
    (90) The Mill Moat House (c. 1820) (91) Holywood Abattoir (c. 1850)

LIII Rockport House, 15 Rockport Road BT18 0DE   85
    (Now Rockport School)
    (92) The House (c. 1840)

CONTENTS

LIV	Seapark Cottage, Seapark Road BT18 ODA (Now Seapark Court and Seapark Mews) (93) The Cottage (c. 1900)	86
LV	Sorrento, Glen Road BT18 OHB (Now Ulster Transport Museum) (94) The House (c. 1875)	87
LVI	Spafield, High Street BT18 9HJ (Now Spafield Fold) (95) The Terrace (1832)	88
LVII	Stanley House, Church Road BT18 9BZ (Now Marmion Adolescent Unit Grounds) (96) The House (1858)	89
LVIII	St. Helen's, 155 High Street BT18 9LG (97) The House (1876) (98) Abbeyfield (1903)	90
LIX	The Firs, 160 High Street BT18 9IIT (now headquarters of C.C.M.S.) (99) The Firs (1889) (100) Gate Lodge (1889)	91
LX	The Vicarage 93 Church Road BT18 9BY (Extant) (Windsor Avenue Development) (101) The Vicarage (1872)	92
LXI	Willesden, 75 Church Road BT18 9BY (Now Development Site) (102) The House (c. 1860)	93
LXII	Woodville 1 and 3 Demesne Road BT18 9DQ (Now Development Site) (103) The Houses (c. 1860)	94
LXIII	Examples of Holywood Gate Piers	95
LXIV	Final Comments (104) and (105) Numbers 9 to 15 Bangor Road (Extant)	

CONTENTS

LXV Glossary   98

LXVI Index   103

Dates given above represent portrayal of the houses in that year, not necessarily the year in which the properties were built. Frequently they were refurbished, sometimes on several occasions. Building dates are given in the text. P.D.L. means Present Day Location. A.P.D.L. means Approximate Present Day Location.

Illustrations from 'Forgotten Houses' and 'Holywood Then and Now' may be obtained from the publisher. The pictures are full colour, signed and mounted, copies of the watercolours on which the illustrations are based.

THE FORGOTTEN HOUSES OF HOLYWOOD
A FEW WORDS BY WAY OF INTRODUCTION

My research for *"Holywood Then and Now"* (Spectator ISBN 0-9542274-09 March 2002), turned up so much relevant information that the Holywood saga requires a few additional pages!

"Forgotten Houses of Holywood" records sketches and stories of local family homes which have been demolished, converted for other purposes or altered from the original building. I hope each essay will be of interest in its own right! Although Holywood's recorded history dates back to A.D. 642, over thirteen hundred years ago, our *"Big Houses"* came within the nineteenth century – only a couple of hundred years ago. I should say mainly came with the nineteenth century, because the origins of Ballymenoch House and Holywood House are attributed to the eighteenth century and Cultra Manor to the early years of the twentieth century. The ten decades between witnessed a massive domestic building programme along the Lough Shore from Tillysburn to Helen's Bay.

The owners or tenants of these fine houses were the business and professional families who moved out from the city to the seaside Mecca, facilitated by better roads and means of transport.

The Holywood tragedy lies in the fact that many of the splendid residences have been demolished. Those which remain must be preserved as an integral part of our heritage. It is unfortunate that present planning regulations pecuniarily encourage demolition in preference to refurbishment. Perhaps community agitation to designate High Holywood, Cultra and Craigavad as areas of special townscape character would preserves what remains in those townlands where exceptionally fine Victorian buildings are extant.

The nineteenth century building extravaganza produced local specialists; builders William Nimick and William Miller, both of the High Street, and Samuel Moore of Morrow's Lane. William Hayes of Marino was the Master Stuccoer who produced the moulded cornices and ceiling roses for which Holywood is famous. Architects whose work appeared in the area were Sir Charles Lanyon, W.H. Lynn, Thomas Hevey, Thomas Turner, John Nash, Messrs Watt and Tulloch, Messrs Young and MacKenzie, W.J. Barre and John Lanyon.

The set of maps and the Bibliography for *"Forgotten Houses"* are identical with the companion volume *"Holywood Then and Now"*. The trilogy will be completed with a review similar to *"Forgotten Houses"* – a collection of essays on Holywood houses extant.

Read and enjoy! Let me have your comments when we meet on Holywood High Street.

Con Auld

I. ABINGDON (1899) P.D.L. 43 DEMESNE ROAD, BT18 9EX

The grounds of Abingdon had entrances into Lemonfield and Demesne Road and was a part of the extremely complex Lot 112 when the town was put for sale by the Harrison family in 1917. Originally the Lot described 20 acres held under conveyance in fee dated 2 September 1708. An 1892 lease named C.K. Cordner, (First) John Harrison (Second) and D Dixon (Third Part). By 1917 the representatives of D. Dixon were the tenants of Lot 112.

Sir Daniel Dixon, M.P., P.C., D.L., J.P. (1844-1907) hailed from Larne. In 1889 he acquired the damaged Holywood Pier, the shoreline to Clanbrassil, Ballymenoch House and its Demesne. Three years later he purchased a major interest in Lot 112 which sprawled over 30 acres of land around Alexandra Avenue (My Lady's Mile) and brought an income of about £150 per annum. Sir Daniel was Belfast's first Lord Mayor and held the mayoralty on five occasions. Apparently he was keen to make his mark on Holywood as well as Belfast!

Abingdon was built in 1899 by Henry Davis. The house was an excellent example of the Arts and Crafts movement. This was an activity of the late nineteenth and early twentieth centuries, in Britain and U.S.A., which stressed the value of artisanship. The arts and architectural guilds felt that the growth of industry and the increasing tendency towards machine production was threatening the quality and individuality of the applied arts in general. The movement sought to unite the decorative arts in a common excellence of design and traditional workmanship. William Morrice (1834-96) supplied a socialist purpose and a pseudo-medieval bias.

Abingdon was acquired by the Potter family and then by Mrs E. McEneaney, who refurbished the house as a competent private nursing home.

The fine entrance gates on Demesne Road were constructed from the hull of famous old ship 'Ark Royal'.

The house was half-timbered above the brick ground floor walls, with string courses. The cornered bay windows and tall timbered gables, all surmounted with hipknobs, were distinctive. The gabled hall was set diagonally and contained an elaborate door case. The first floor windows carried angled arches, those in the staircase gable were exceptionally fine. All barge boards were joined with struts set off the walls. The chimney stacks were diagonally set on plinths.

Abingdon was needlessly demolished in 1995 during the night prior to the Borough Council meeting on which its listing was to be ratified. The two acre site was used to erect the five dwellings call *"Demesne Close"*.

Here are some other examples of the Arts and Crafts movement in Holywood.

The Almshouses (Downshire Road (Q.V.)
Ardmoyle (Clanbrassil Road)
Derryquin (Old Cultra Avenue)
King Edward VII Memorial Hall (Sullivan Place)
Masonic Hall (Sullivan Place)
Rayanne House (Demesne Road)
Redclyffe (Police Service, High Street). Redclyffe was build in 1889 for Dr. David Johnston. In 1934 it was acquired by the Police Service. It is a chaste brick building with sandstone dressings, elliptical windows and excellent interior woodwork. Unfortunately the fine stained-glass staircase window "went missing" during a refurbishment.

Sands Soldiers Home (demolished, Strathern Court)
St. Valentines (Upper Church Road). St. Valentines was built in 1897. It was destroyed by fire in the 1980's. The extensive site was used for the most prestigious suite of domestic residences erected in Holywood in the second half of the twentieth century.

The Firs (Belfast Road) (Q.V.).

Abingdon

St Valentines

II AGRICULTURAL COLLEGE (1849) P.D.L. 93A 95 VICTORIA ROAD, BT18 9BG

Miss McAlester, daughter of the Rev Charles McAlester and his wife Rachel, a very old lady in 1924, remembered Holywood when she was a little girl in 1850. *"Croft Road was a lane with no houses except a farm where Croft House is today; it belonged to Mrs McKibben and later to the ancestors of the Ballagh Family. An Agricultural School had been built in 1849 beyond this farm, unfortunately it did not flourish and the building was converted into two houses, Burnleigh and Crofton".*

I have recorded the story of the County Down Agricultural College in the companion volume *"Holywood Then and Now"*. Suffice to say here that in 1837 the National Commissioners' report on Education required that in each of the 25 districts an Agricultural School and Model Farm be established. Dr. McKittrick, Medical Officer for Holywood, obtained the preferred Government grant for the town.

The school, which could accommodate 100 students, was opened on Ballykeel Road beside the Stinking Burn (today's location is the corner of Victoria Road and Croft Road).

The model farm covered seven Cunningham Acres and occupied the present day site of Croft and Brook House. For information I include a comparison of acre sizes as designed by Thomas Bain of the Royal Academical Institution.

(A) Irish or Plantation Acre   7840 sq. yards
(B) Scottish or Cunningham Acre 6250 sq. yards
(C) English or Imperial acre 4840 sq. yards

The Agricultural College did not attract sufficient students to make it viable. The Inspector's report to the commissioners (31 October 1851) stated *"The school is valueless, possibly injurious and certainly a waste of public money".* The County Down Agricultural College closed its doors at the end of summer term, June 1852.

The Nine Bay, two storeyed building had a central gable with entrance doors. The windows were eight paned and carried label mouldings; possibly the quoins are original. The Agricultural College was rather reminiscent of the old parochial National School Building opposite the Parish Church (1845).

In the 1850's the superfluous Agriculture College became semi-detached villa residences. Wings were added to each end of the long narrow building, the central entrance was closed and each house gained an elaborately decorated entrance porch with cusped barge boards and hipknobs, similar ornaments appear at the other gables.

Redesign of interiors was achieved expertly, although a few signs of the former educational establishment are evident. The staircases maintain the mien of an institution rather than a spacious Victorian villa. The former entrance hall area remains in one house, whereas its first storey equivalent is within the neighbouring house. The upper frames of windows in the additional wings have slightly curved heads whereas those in the original building are square headed.

Considerable interior decoration was added, extensive stucco work, moulded skirtings, architraves and woodwork. The old school house was converted with such expertise that it is difficult to recognise the original purpose of these grade "A" Victorian period residences.

Agricultural College

Burnleigh & Crofton

III. ALMA TERRACE (1858) BT18 9DP – P.D.L. 23-25 CHURCH VIEW
NOW HARBINSON MEWS

Church view presumably got its name after the Parish Church removed from the Priory to its present location in 1844. Before that year the lane was the north boundary of the Commons, which extended to the present day Demesne Road.

Demesne Road dates from the mid 1830's; it continued across Downshire Road, then a country pathway, through Lemonfield to the Shepherd's Path (now My Lady's Lane).

Alma Terrace is marked on the 1859 Ordnance Survey map. By that year the Commons are shown as long ribbons of land extending to the north boundary of the Parish Church grounds. Miss McAllester tells us *"colloquially the area was known as the backs of the gardens and a double ditch ran parallel to Church view"*.

Alma Terrace contained only two houses. Number 25 had a double bay extending to the roof at about a foot from the main building. This had a wide coach arch leading through to a courtyard at the rear. Number 23 had three bays. All the windows were square pane and doors were panelled.

On the opposite side of Church View, in the 1800's, Dennis Sullivan, brother of Dr. Robert Sullivan acquired one of the ribbons of land on the Commons. He built the dubiously named "Seaview Terrace" on the site, as well as other houses on Church View.

Alma Terrace was simple and sturdy with unpainted stucco and was well maintained. Number 23 was needlessly demolished in 1973, its site lay vacant for many years, overgrown with weeds and collecting rubbish. Number 25 was demolished in 1999 and the four apartments known as Harbinson Mews built on the site in 2001.

IV ALMSHOUSES (1913) P.D.L. 108-114 DOWNSHIRE ROAD BT18 9LZ

Holywood has an alternative history connected with the Great War through "Woodbine Willie". Rev. G.A. Studdert Kennedy was the famous army padre who brought solace to wounded soldiers in the trenches and hospital wards with Woodbine cigarettes and sympathetic conversation. "Woodbine Willey" was a kinsman of Rev. L.S. Kennedy, Vicar of Holywood from 1864 to 1869.

Rev. Lancelot Studdert Kennedy (1831-1899) hailed from County Offaly. His father was Rev. Robert Mitchell Kennedy, Dean of Clonfert. His mother was Anne Studdert from the County Clare. Lancelot entered Trinity College, Dublin in 1850 and was ordained Deacon in 1860 and priest in 1891. He was appointed Assistant Curate of Holywood Parish in 1860 and Vicar, following the death of Rev. H.E. Crutwell in 1864.

Lancelot married Katherine Louisa Oulton, daughter of the Garrison Chaplain of Belfast. Her grandfather was Rev. George MaCartney who had been Vicar of Holywood from 1770 to 1773. It seems Rev. Dr. George MaCartney was a man of considerable virility, holding five livings at the same time, between 1805 and 1813, as well as being a Justice of the Peace in Antrim.

During the ministry of Rev. L.S. Kennedy enlargement of the Church building commenced in December 1867, the graveyard was extended in 1866 and at Westminster, discussion took place leading towards a Bill to disestablish the State Church (April 1869). Vicar Kennedy resigned the living in January 1869 and continued his service in the Established Church of England until his retirement in 1899.

Although he became Rector of Newdigate in Surrey he returned to Holywood for his wedding and the baptism of both his sons. He died in Holywood on 4 July 1899 and was interred in the Old Priory Graveyard. The congregation erected a memorial tablet to Rev. Lancelot Studdert Kennedy in the Chancel. His widow, Katherine Louisa Kennedy, donated the four Almshouses to the congregation in memory of her husband.

The four cottages have the appearance of the Arts and Crafts movement. The Downshire Road facades combine red brick ground floor with white stucco first storey. The roof of the hall and half bay window extension have exposed rafter ends below fascias. In each, the roof proper is similarly finished. The panelled front doors have fan lights and the first storey sash windows have double lights. Today the Almshouses are in private ownership.

V. ALTONA (C. 1895) P.D.L. 69 CHURCH ROAD BT18 9BX

By a lease of Mayday 1894, annual rent £5, James Beggs Esq. was required to build one dwelling house with poor law valuation of not less than £25 and within twelve months from date of the lease. The house had to be set back one hundred feet from the Church Road; the space in front had to be used as an ornamental garden or shrubbery. *"Exposure of Clothes"* was forbidden – a usual condition in Harrison Estate leases. It seems the Squire had an aversion to viewing Monday morning washing hanging on Holywood lines!

No nuisance was allowed, no unhealthy trade or dangerous occupation would be tolerated in the new house. Also, the premise was not to be used as a public house. It seems the Harrison's were very careful when it came to granting leases for buildings beside the local places of worship – especially the Parish Church, which they attended every Sabbath day!

In the 1917 sale of head-rents, the half-acre Altona site was offered subject to such rights of way, rights to light and air and other easements as legally existed.

Accordingly Altona was built where it would not obscure the pleasant view of the Lanyon designed Parish Church.

Space remained towards the west boundary for a large orchard, and kitchen garden.

The house looked much older than its (almost) twentieth century date, when compared with St. Valentines, situated further up the Church Road Hill, which was built about the same time as Altona.

The neo-classical façade encouraged the impression of *"James Beggs' Sensible Square House"*. The Irish pilaster quoins led up to the more usual indented quoins of the first floor. The door case and window surrounds were elaborate. String courses surrounded the building. Full plate glazing in the high sash windows indicated the more recent date of the house.

James Begg's daughter continued to live in Altona until the 1970's, when it was acquired as a residence for the curates of the Parish Church. In the mid 1980's it became a private residential home providing care for elderly and retired Holywood folk. Later Altona was extensively refurbished, before it got a new lease of life as an exclusive guesthouse.

In 2000 the fine old building was demolished, to make way for two modern apartment buildings. These incorporate the roof pattern of the neighbouring Lanyon designed Church. A few of the Beggs family specimen trees are carefully preserved.

Altona Manor contains twelve apartments, to the west Altona Lodge provides an additional five apartments.

VI ARDTULLAGH (C.1850) P.D.L. REDBURN COUNTRY PARK AT JUNCTION OF DEMESNE ROAD, OLD HOLYWOOD ROAD AND JACKSON'S ROAD BT18 9QH

Ardtullagh had the appearance of a mid-nineteenth century mansion. It was built within a section of the estate which became Redburn after the Dunville family removed there from Richmond (1867) (Q.V.). A wide and straight bridle path joined the two mansions, along which the equestrian Dunville family exercised their horses and hounds.

In the 1917 sale of the town only part of the grounds appeared under the first lot. That was an area of 2 acres covering the carriage avenue and the Little Combe behind the house.

Apparently Ardtullagh was inhabited by a succession of tenants. William Anketell, Chairman of the Belfast and County Down Railway was an early resident.

In 1884 Captain John Harrison was living in Ardtullagh. The Harrisons of Holywood House (Q.V.) and Mertoun Hall (Q.V.) were squires of Holywood, after they acquired the town from the Kennedy Estate in 1854. This may explain why the Spectator Newspaper (incorrectly) refers to Ardtullagh as a Manor House (Edition 11 February 1956). In 1886 Rev. F.M. Scott was in residence.

The following year (1887) the Church of Ireland authorities sold 'Ashfield', The Bishop's Palace (Q.V.) to the War Department for military use. The Rt. Rev. Dr. Thomas

Old Clubhouse

James Welland, and Bishop of Down, Connor and Dromore came to Ardtullagh in 1892 and removed to Culloden (Q.V.) in 1899.

Sir George Clark (Workman and Clark Shipbuilders) and his family came to live in the big house in the early years of last century. During the Second World War it was requisitioned by the Royal Air Force and Women's Auxiliary Air Force and immediately a village of wooden huts sprang up around the Ardtullagh.

The neighbouring property on the east boundary was Holywood Golf Club. On 15 October 1945 the Clubhouse, situated on the Nun's Walk, was destroyed by fire. The member's took up residence in the recently vacated Ardtullagh – a mere third of a mile to the west. The beautiful old house was refurbished and became a commodious and prestigious clubhouse. The members returned to the Nun's Walk site, where a purpose-build clubhouse was opened in 1962.

The Holywood Urban District Council had acquired the Dunville Estate in 1950. At reorganisation of Local Government in 1972 Ardtullagh became the property of the Department of the Environment. The estate became Redburn Country Park.

Although one important facet of D.O.E. is the preservation of our heritage and important buildings,

Ardtullagh

Ardtullagh was needlessly demolished. Holywood Plan Draft, Map One, Study (November 1977) shows the M3 running directly over the site of Ardtullagh House. At the beginning of the twenty first century the area of the fine old mansion is maintained as a lawn at the top of the third of a mile long avenue. Parts of the old wooden entrance gateposts are extant.

The house was square with a hipped roof. Various offices extended to the rear beyond a central enclosed courtyard. A one storey wing extended to the east which conveniently served as the professional's shop and office when Ardtullagh was a golf club house. The semi-circular headed windows had drip courses, string courses connected the bracketed cills. These, with the quoins and roof cornice, were carved from honey coloured sand stone.

The plain four bay north facing façade commanded a splendid view over the lough, the east facing entrance front had an elaborate door case with extensive mouldings. The big house fitted like a glove unto its wooded hillside park.

Before turning to the story of "Ardville" I shall include to a couple of 'forgotten houses' in the Ardtullagh area.

On the 200 feet contour line at the top of the Nun's Walk, the greens' Keeper of the Holywood Golf Club lived in a delightful little cottage. It was symmetrical three bay, the central symmetrical jamb wall supporting a tall brick chimney. A lattice work porch had been added at some time, which I seem to remember was covered with red roses in

summertime. The gabled roof had exposed rafter ends, foiled barge boards and hipknobs. Traditionally it was the site of the cell of a self-martyring nun. (See 'Holywood Then and Now').

Further up the hill, directly behind the cottage on the 500 feel contour line Holywood Hill House dominated the skyline. It was a large symmetrical five bay farmhouse which semi circular headed windows in the gables. The farm was approached from the Moss Road (BT18 9RU) and had a wide range of agricultural buildings towards the entry lane. The house was destroyed by fire. Today it is a gaunt ghostly ruin surrounded by heaps of stones through which the winds whistle during every seasons of the year. However, the view is spectacular!

VII. ARDVILLE (BEFORE 1820) P.D.L. OLD QUAY ROAD AND FARMHILL ROAD, BT18 0AL

The original building, possibly a farm house, dated back to the early years of the nineteenth century. About 1840 a grand mansion, in the Irish Georgian style, was added towards the north front, after part of the old house had been removed.

Before mid-century, Theodore Bozi was in residence, he had removed from Belfast's Antrim Road to Ardville to join the growing population of *"Linen Barons"* of the nineteenth century Holywood scenario.

Theodore Bozi brought considerable kudos to the neighbourhood, as he was the Spanish Consul. Perhaps his life style accounts for the considerable alterations to Ardville, which took place about that time.

By 1852 James Lennon had brought his family to live in Ardville. He was a shipowner, ships' chandler and manufacturer of ships' ropes and canvas, located in nautical Corporation Square, Belfast.

In 1875 James Barbour (1836-1907) was living in Ardville. By that time the local railway station had been built on the Holywood to Bangor extension line (inaugurated 18 May 1865). It was given the name 'Marino' – possibly after the neighbouring Marino Farm; soon the surrounding houses added 'Marino' to the prestigious address.

James was a member of the Barbour Family of linen-thread renown, and brother-in-law to James Combe, founder of the world famous Falls Foundry. The foundry covered five acres, employed fifteen hundred mechanics and was world leader in manufacture of machinery for the textile industry. Combe, Barbour and Combe Ltd. claimed the earliest installation of electricity in the Province.

Surgeon Kelly (1850) commented on Ardville *"Next to Marino House is the residence of Theodore Bozi the Spanish Council at Belfast. The House is of modern structure and beautifully situated, occupying part of the extensive Cultra Demesne".* An excellent illustration of "Ardville" appears on the entrepreneurial pictorial map (c. 1865) *"Houses and Building Sites to be let at Cultra".*

Originally the grounds of Ardville lay between the boundary with the Prairie – (now called the Priory) – and the seashore, they were bisected by the Quay Road. Old Quay Road acquired its present name in the 1960's when the Post Office required street numbers to be scribed on envelopes, formerly it was known as "The Lane". The first Ordance Survey Map (1834) shows a road running from Cultra Quay to the quarry at Cultra Point, thence approximately via Clanbrassil Road, to the Belfast Road. Produce for and from Holywood used the road. The front façade of the main house has a pillared bow-fronted central bay surmounted with an elaborate over-panel above a heavily mounded cornice and blocking course which surrounds the roof. Ground floor windows are semi-circular headed with drip courses, as are the blind window and door case of the large balustraded entrance porch.

The interior of the mansion continues the external splendour. From the entrance hall, which extends through the full height of the building, a fine staircase leads to the upper floors. The window and door cases are notable, as are the marble mantle pieces and stuccowork.

Formerly behind the house there were kitchen gardens, green houses and stove houses including a small cottage which opened unto Farmhill Road. The front tennis and croquet lawns descended to the porters lodge, which is extant but greatly enlarged

Geoffrey Garrod M.A. Principal of The Royal Belfast Academical Institution, retired to Ardville in 1938, he was the last owner to enjoy utility of the entire Mansion House. After the Second World War Ardville was acquired "For A Song". At the auction of the Garrod family effects, the Bechstein grand piano went for another melody! (Ten pounds).

Soon the house was divided into three sections. 1. Ardville – the domestic wing, possibly the original farmhouse; 2. Wind Rush – the main house, built about 1840; 3, Ardreagh – the servants wing opening unto Farmhill Road through a small gate in the high stone wall. Since then other buildings have been added and parts of the grounds have been divided into sites for modern houses.

Fortunately, the sea meadow was acquired by the North Down Borough Council and added to Sea Park Recreation Grounds – otherwise it would have been covered with houses.

The small postern which opened at Clanbrassil Corner is extant. The customary grand entrance was not built, instead wooded gates accompanied by picket fencing opened unto Old Quay Road.

Ardville remains into the twenty-first century, greatly altered. The surrounding contemporary properties, Marino House, Farmhill, Ward's Cottages, The Prairie, the Coast Guard Station and the Station Master's house are unspoiled and continue to be inhabited as family homes. I hope to include their stories in a complementary volume describing the extant houses of Holywood.

Ardville

VIII. ASHFIELD, THE BISHOP'S PALACE (1827) A.P.D.L. BELFAST ROAD, PALACE BARRACKS BT18 9QY

Ashfield was built by Rt. Rev. Richard Mant, 63rd Bishop of Down, to which the Diocese of Connor had been added in 1451 and Dromore in 1842. Before coming to Holywood in 1823, he had been Bishop of Killaloe (1820-1823). A lease dated 12 February 1827 was acquired from John Jackson and a palace fit for a Lord Bishop of the Established Church, was soon designed for the site.

Richard Mant was an Englishman who though himself *"A Perfect Stranger to the New Diocese"* which he considered to be *"The most eligible in the country; County Down resembling many parts of England"*.

Holywood was a Presbyterian town, the new Bishop observed the fraternisation between Anglicans and Dissenters, which his predecessor, Bishop Nathanael Alexander, had encouraged before his translation to Meath. Bishop Mant was determined to terminate such mutual accommodation. At that time there was a growing propensity towards regeneration in all Irish denominations. In Holywood the movement led to a spate of modern Church building projects. Lack of sensibility, misunderstandings of the Ulster life-style and *"High Church"* opinions brought Richard Mant into conflict with clergy and laity alike.

His memorial is *"The Alpha and Omega"* window in the Parish Church. Such was the builder of the palace.

Bishop Mant's successor was a happy contrast. Rt. Rev. Robert Knox became Bishop of Down, Connor and Dromore in May 1849, and lived in the palace until he was elected Archbishop of Armagh in 1886. The Knox family was involved in every aspect of Holywood life. Townfolk of every persuasion rejoiced in his many successes and were sorry to see the family leave for Armagh city. The Archbishop's funeral to the Priory in 1893 was the largest procession Holywood had ever seen. The *"Little Children"* window in the south aisle of the Parish Church is in memory of Archbishop Knox. Three other windows are memorials to the family.

Rt. Rev. William Reeves came to the see in 1886 and choose to reside in Conway House, Dunmurry.

The Palace was sold by public auction in the Rosemary Street sale rooms of H and C Clarke. The new owner was the War Office of Her Majesty's Government. The army had been using the Kinnegar Camp as a training ground for Belfast Regiments since the 1880's. In 1887 the War Office bought part of the Kinnegar from the Harrison estate. The inclement weather and flooding of those years made the resident regiments appreciate the high ground of the new Palace Camp.

The army demolished the house and stables in 1890; the present day clock tower marks the site of the old palace.

Surgeon Kelly (1850) recorded *"The grounds which surround the See-House, although not extensive or marked by any attractive object of interest, seem to have been judiciously arranged in accordance with the style and extent of the mansion, which is free from any architectural effect. It can only convey to the visitor the impression of the abode of a private country gentleman than the palace of a noble prelate of three of the most important dioceses in Ireland"*.

M.M. Kertland (1834) Ordnance Survey notes *"Ashfield, the residence of the Bishop of Down and Connor, is situated in the town land of Knocknagoney. The palace is handsome, though not large and the plantations around it are not extensive"*.

Ashfield was "H" shaped with a colonnaded porch set into the five bay recess of the entrance front. A shaded patio was provided on the west façade and adequate stabling and horticultural offices extended with the courtyard from the back of the house which lacked the ornamentation of buildings erected in the following decades. The reception rooms enjoyed a splendid view over the Kinnegar to the lough.

The contemporary Gate Lodge on Belfast Road was demolished in 1890. Westbrook, the neighbouring mansion, was demolished to enlarge the Palace Military Barracks campus. It was built in 1817 by Rev. Edward May, the Sovereign of Belfast. The grounds of Westbrook bordered the west side of Jackson's Road; its entrance and lodge were replaced by the Linley Gates. Both Ashfield and Westbrook were part of the Jackson family farmstead, the best known member of which was Thomas Jonathan Jackson (1824-1893) U.S. Confederacy General.

All that remains of the palace are several large ornamental urns. These were used in the bishops' gardens; today they serve a similar purpose in gardens on Victoria Road and at Port Braddan on the Causeway Coast.

The Bishop's Palace

IX. BATH COTTAGE A.P.D.L. STRAND AVENUE BT18 9AW, HOLYWOOD THROUGHPASS

Lot 82 in the 1917 sale of the town covered about forty buildings, including
(1) Bath Cottage, the tenant of which at that time was William Martin, by lease from Henry Harrison.
(2) The land around Johnny the Jig Playground and Robert Sullivan's birthplace, the tenant was W McCormick by lease from Dorothea Kennedy.
(3) The Belfast Bar, tenant Jonathan Jefferson by lease of Simon Issac to John Rowley.
(4) The Bath houses, the old Presbyterian Church, the Kirk session house, Lennox Place and Stewart's Place Cottage. Tenants W. McCormick and Mrs O'Kane, the latter having a lease from John Harrison.

Here is the story of old Holywood and its proprietors in a nut shell, centred around the Strand (Gospel Lane), Stewart's Palace, Bath Terrace and the seashore. This was before the intrusion of the railway embankment in 1865, the Northern Ireland Housing Trust in 1967 and the Through Pass in the 1970's.

The Presbyterian Church, built in 1750 for the removal of the congregation from the Sea-Meadows, was rectangular, with three entrances and steps leading to the

(Old Presbyterian Kirk)

galleries. It had seating for 735 adherents. When the congregation removed to the new church on Bangor Road in 1842, the building was used as a Masonic Hall and a mission station for the Episcopal Church. The Kirk Session House trebled as local courtroom and goal.

The Belfast Bar (Old Priory Inn) dates back to 1840; its history is recorded in "Holywood, Then and Now". The Bath Houses were operated by John Rowley and his daughter Anne. Hugh Stewart, who developed most of this area for the tourist trade, ran a second bathhouse. Dr. Robert Sullivan's birth place is marked by the prestigious blue plaque of the Ulster History Circle

Bath Cottage was built about the year 1850. The terrace in which it was situated stretched along the sea wall to meet Shore Street at Shore Field Coastguard Station. The cottage was two storey, four bay symmetrical terrace style, its windows had margined glazing bars. At some time a semi-hexagonal porch had been added, no doubt to protect the front door from storms and high seas, as the cottage was situated a few meters from high tide mark.

Surgeon Kelly refers to Bath Terrace as *"Affording respectable family apartments for visitors to Holywood, during the summer holiday season"*. Today nothing of the Strand remains except a name and the memory of a village within a town.

Bath Cottage

Stewarts Place Cottage

Ballymenoch House c1825

X   BALLYMENOCH HOUSE P.D.L. BALLYMENOCH PARK AND SALVATION ARMY RESIDENTIAL HOME, BANGOR ROAD, BT18 0LQ

In 1611 the Plantation Commissioners reported *"Sr. James Hamylton is preparing to build a house at Hollywood, three miles from Bangor; and two hundred thousand of bricks with other materials ready at the place, where there are some 20 houses inhabited with English and Scottes"*. J.W. Kernothan, Holywood's late eighteenth century antiquarian claimed this *"House at Hollywood"* was the original building on the Ballymenoch site. He pointed out that a branch of the Hamilton family had lived there right up to the end of the eighteenth century. Their funerary monument was removed from the Priory Graveyard to the proprietary chapel at Clandeboye, by the Marquees of Dufferin and Ava.

Possibly the old house was refurbished towards the end of the eighteenth century. E. R. Proctor in his *"Belfast Scenery"* (1832) depicts a square, two storey building with tripartite windows and a portico.

Around the turn into the nineteenth century the Holmes family was in residence. The best known member of the family was Robert Holmes, the famous Irish Barrister. A quotation from Surgeon Kelly (1850) reads *"we shall tarry at Ballymenock the beautiful residence of Thomas Gregg., It is extensive and although bears a modern aspect, yet it is among the most ancient family residences in the parish. It was built, we believe by Mr Holmes, a near relative of the father of the Irish bar. It is only a matter of respect that the*

proprietor has closed from the public such a delightful haunt. However, the richness and elegance of the mansion and its grounds fulfil the promise of the fine gates and embossed columns at the entrance".

In 1802 the Ballymenoch estate was acquired by Cunningham Greg, a wealthy Belfast merchant. He was a founder member of the Academical Institution and used his right to sponsor the nineteen year old Robert Sullivan for a scholarship. He was gratified to receive a sonnet on Ballymenoch House from the young poet. Thomas Richard Greg J.P. (1805-1884) succeeded his father and acted as one of the executors of Dr. Sullivan's testament, which made provisions for the poor of Holywood and the Sullivan Schools.

Rev. W.A. Holmes, (1819) Vicar of Holywood during Robert Sullivan's adolescent years, in his statistical account of the parish recorded *"Ballymena, the residence of Cunningham Greg is a large and modern structure. The offices are remarkably extensive and the shubbery is said to excel anything of the kind in the North of Ireland".*

Sir Daniel Dixon M.P. P.C. D.L. J.P. (1844-1907) bought the estate in 1889. At the same time he acquired the burnt shell of the famous Holywood pier and sea-board property as far as Clanbrassil Terrace. Sir Daniel was Belfast's first Lord Major (1888) and served in the mayoralty on five

occasions. Educated at "Inst" his main interests lay in shipping and transport. He served as High Sheriff and received a barony in 1903. (Also See Abingdon (Q.V).

In 1913 Ballymenoch House was destroyed by fire. Sir Samuel Kelly, ship-owner and coal importer, rebuilt the house and improved the parklands. Sir Samuel and Lady Mary Kelly were exuberant supporters of many Holywood organisations, especially the Yacht Club.

After her husband's death, Lady Mary built Woodlands (later called Ardtullagh) at Crawfordsburn. The Holywood residence was donated to the Salvation Army and became the enterprising Eventide Home, which provides a very useful service to the community. In 1953 the twenty-one acres of pleasure gardens were given to the people of Holywood, for use as a public park.

At both entrances there were pretty little "ink-pot" lodges, elliptical with conical roofs rising to tall circular stone chimney stacks. J.A.K. Dean (1994) dates them about 1805. The main lodge was demolished c. 1930 and the Marino Lodge in 1971, when the road to Bangor was widened. Beside the Marino Gate a pleasant wide porticoed cottage was demolished at the same time.

Fortunately road-works did not vandalise the mansion's ice-house. It remains extract on the bank above the Ballymenoch Burn at the place formerly called *"Ice-House Corner"*.

A furlong to the south of the Mansion House lay an extensive market garden, the high stone walls of which

Bangor Gate Lodge

sheltered a long range of stove and glass houses. The garden and greenhouses produced vegetables, flowers and fruit for the house and the town. Ballymenoch peaches were eagerly sought for the tables of the Grand Central Hotel in Belfast.

Around this complex was accommodation for members of the Ballymenoch staff. Today Croft Park and Croft Close cover the sites of the stable yard and the market gardens.

Beyond the Court Yard and further up Ballymenoch Hill on King John's Road, an estate cottage was used as a mass-house when the Greg's family was living in the Mansion House. Mass was celebrated in Jeremiah Lockhart's house before St. Patrick's Church was consecrated in 1829. Jeremiah was one of the gardeners who carefully tended the broad and beautiful acres of Ballymenoch House.

Garden Facade c 1912

Estate cottages at Marino

XI   BROOKLYN (C.1850) P.D.L. 69-75 VICTORIA ROAD, BT18 9BG

Brooklyn is one of the forgotten houses of Holywood of which neither photograph nor painting is available. The sketch which accompanies the article is based upon large scale Ordnance Survey (1/1250) and the few people who remember the fire which consumed the house in the early 1930's.

All the town crowded Victoria Road and the Twistle Bridge pathway for a grandstand view of the spectacular fireworks display. In those days houses were illuminated by gaslight, candles and oil lamps. Conflagrations were frequent. As a point of interest I shall include a list of Holywood premises destroyed by fire (E.A. = Enemy Action)

usual string courses, hipped roofs to the entrance front, gabled to the rear.

Ordnance Survey maps shown two other buildings by the riverside, a tennis court and grounds sprawling over the gardens of the present day numbers 69 to 75 Victoria Road. The piers are extant and give entry to number 69. A series of paths and steps appear to have provided one of the most beautiful riverside properties in High Holywood.

Among the families which lived in Brooklyn were the Keegans the Clellands and possibly the Collins family.

Since the fire, the site had accommodated four

1. Holywood Pier
2. Holywood Town Hall
3. Ballymenoch House (Q.V.)
4. St. Valentines (Q.V.)
5. Mertoun Hall (Q.V.)
6. Maryfield (Q.V.)
7. Redburn (Q.V.)
8. Clanbrassil Villa (Q.V.)
9. Clanbrassil Terrace (No. 1) Q.V.
10. 25 Clanbrassil Road (E.A.)
11. 2 & 4 Ailsa Road (E.A.)
12. 49 Victoria Road (Restored)
13. Holywood Railway Station
14. St. Colmcilles Church
15. Olave Hall (Guides) Park Drive
16. Priory Church (Roof, 1572)
17. Holywood Hill House (Q.V.)
18. Knocknatten (Roof)
19. Swiss Chalet (16 Farmhill Road)
20. Old Palace Bar (E.A.)
21. Benedar, Seapark (Restored)
22. Loughview Hotel (E.A.)
23. Methodist Church Vergers Residence
24. Maypole Cinema
25. Meneelys Garage on High St.
26. Holywood Players Hall, High Street.

Brooklyn was built shortly after 1850, on the banks of the Ballykeel River. It displayed two stories to the entrance front and three to the river front.

It appears to have been a large rambling house made up of several unusual angled bays on the façade to Victoria Road, the front door was included within a canted bay with double openings on either side and single openings in each of the cants. Other openings led to a canted corner to the north façade. Those who remember the house think the windows carried semi-circular heads with drip courses, the

handsome villa residences each tastefully surrounded by well-kept riverside gardens, one of which has pedestrian entrance with foot bridge across the Ballykeel River to Church Avenue.

Perhaps one day a more accurate account and picture of Brooklyn with the story of its residents may become available.

XII CLANBRASSIL TERRACE (2-6 CLANBRASSIL ROAD BT18 OAP)

Entrepreneurs George McAuliffe and James Connor commissioned cartographer J. Phillips to draw a pictorial map of houses and building sites to be let along the coast, shortly after the arrival of the Belfast and Bangor Railway Company at Marino and Cultra stations.

Clanbrassil Terrace is depicted as having five houses. Those at the ends are built at right angles to the central block. The house at the west end was destroyed by fire in 1878. The proposed house at the east end was not completed, protruding building stones indicated the intended additional residence.

Accompanying stabling accommodation was unnecessary as the developers had reserved a site for *"Stables, offices and yard"* where number 10 Clanbrassil Road is today.

A double banked earth terrace rose from the sea bordered lawns to conceal the basement windows. Tennis courts and a pitch and putt course spread before the entrance front. A driveway was designed to surround the completed terrace. In each of the houses five bays face the sea, two of which are a four openings bay window rising through three stories. The entrance façade is three bay with a large central porch surmounted with urn finals. String course is extravagant. Pebble and small stone surrounds and key-stones to all openings are peculiar to Clanbrassil Terrace. The gabled roof is extended unto elaborate brackets. All this produces an austere town-house appearance to Clanbrassil Road and an attractive sea-side terrace effect to survey the lough shore.

Internally the reception rooms and hallways command views of both seaboard and country. The high ceiling reception rooms display the expert work of stoccoer Willian Hayes of Marino. Although built in 1867, the bathrooms' equipment boasted showers, bidets and every toilet facility of the twenty first century. The basement floors provided full culinary capacity with wine cellars and housekeepers rooms.

Over the years a variety of families lived in the Terrace. Robert Steele (seed importer of Victoria Street) John Morrow (Ulster Tarpaulins of Cromac Square) Captain John Auld (Head Line) John Parker news editor and sports commentator,

My grandparents came to number one in the early years of last century, I was born in the house and enjoyed life there until I went up to University. It was a warm, comfortable friendly family home, as were the other houses in the Terrace.

Holywood is fortunate to retain this fine example of Irish Victorian domestic architecture at its very best.

XIII CLANBRASSIL VILLAS (C.1866) 15 SEAFRONT ROAD BT18 OBB

Like the terrace, Clanbrassil Villas took their name from Henry Hamilton, Earl of Clanbrassil, grandson and last lineal descendent of Sir James Hamilton, the modern proprietor of Holywood. The clan Brazil territories lay on the south east shores of Lough Neagh.

In his map (C1866) J. Phillips depicts Clanbrassil Villa (East) and Clanbrassil Villa (West) situated on a seafront site previously occupied by Cultra Cottage, the residence of Hugh McClelland. At this time both houses appear to be available to rent.

The semi-detached houses were erected in brick with sandstone dressings in 1866 by one of the developers of the area. James Connor, construction and civil engineer of Great George Street in Belfast. The Connor family lived in one of the houses for a decade or so.

After part of the East Villa was destroyed by fire, its sibling acquired additional rooms and a central staircase hall. A sandstone pillar in the sea battery wall indicates the gardens' division between the former semi-detached houses.

Restoration after the fire was achieved with such skill that the reconstructed single residence exhibited few exterior signs of is semi-detached origin. Indeed some commentators claim the villas always had been a single residence!

Sir Charles Blackmore took up residence in 1930. He was secretary to Sir James Craig. Also secretary of the Stormont Government and equerry to King George VI.

In 1967 Sir John Swinson bought Clanbrassil and transformed it into the most prestigious hotel on the lough shores. In 1984 Mrs E.McEneaney acquired the building for use as a private nursing home. It was demolished in 1999 and the site used for Clanbrassil Court, twin apartment blocks built on the seaside site for a dozen fortunate families.

XIV CRAIGAVAD HOUSE
(BEFORE 1783 P.D.L. STATION ROAD BT18 OBP, ROYAL BELFAST GOLF CLUB)

The original Craigavad House dates back to the eighteenth century when the Pottinger Family was in residence (1783). The Pottingers were among the founders of modern Belfast. Thomas was Town Sovereign in 1661; Sir Henry, a Belfast Academy student, became Governor of Hong Kong, Cape of Good Hope and Madras. In 1842 he negotiated the British lease on Hong Kong, at the end of the Chinese opium wars. The family kept their hounds at the Kennel Bridge on the Old Holywood Road. The name Pottinger is memorialised in many Belfast locations.

Sometime before 1817 Arthur Forbes (1781-1847) acquired the house. His uncle John Forbes was a former Governor of the Bahamas and a member of Henry Grattan's Independent Party, determined on Irish Government Reform. An engraving made by a relative of Arthur Forbes, Mrs Todd-Thornton, depicts Craigavad House and surrounding countryside in 1844.

When Arthur Forbes died in 1847, John Mulholland, acquired the property. He built a neo-classical mansion designed by Thomas Turner, on the site of the old house.

John's father, Andrew Mulholland, founded the York Street Flax Spinning and Weaving Company in 1830. Andrew's younger brother St. Clair Kenburne Mulholland acquired "Eglantine" at Hillsborough in 1845.

Andrew Mulholland purchased "Springvale" Ballywalter in 1846. He engaged Charles Lanyon to design the magnificent Ballywalter Park mansion. The wealthy Ulster linen manufacturers were created Barons Dunleath in 1892. John removed to Ballywalter Park, after the death of his father.

The present owners of Craigavad claim that the house was built in the same year as the Club was founded on the Holywood Kinnegar (1881). Afterwards it passed successively into the ownership of Sir. Edward Coey, Sir Edward Porter Cowan, A.Kirker Esq., and Rt. Hon. J.C. White, a former Lord Mayor of Belfast.

Craigavad House is a fine example of the work of Thomas Turner, who served in the office of Sir Charles Lanyon. The house is built in the Neo-Classical style, massive, reserved and impressive when viewed from the Belfast Lough.

The upper storey and wings display the traditional twelve square pane windows with segmentally arched heads. The ground floor carries channelled rustication and a very elaborate pillared porch with heavy balconette. String courses are extravagant and the vast hipped roof has wide eaves with cornice.

The Royal Belfast Golf Club acquired Craigavad House and the 140 acre estate in 1925 for £6,000. Towards this figure the construction of the course and conversion to clubhouse the members subscribed £11,500.

A major refurbishment was undertaken in 1958 costing £40,000. In 1978 the grand central hall rising through the building was incorporated. Today Craigavad House is one of the leading historic clubhouses in the United Kingdom.

Originally there were three lodges, one of which was demolished before 1900. The Belfast Lodge (by Thomas Turner) is Cottage Orné style. It is "T" shaped, a bow-ended wing with projecting semi-conical roof faces the Bangor Road. A gabled hallway with semi circular headed door case, family

crest and quoins, opens unto the vanished driveway to the mansion house.

The Italianate style Bangor Lodge (c. 1851 by Thomas Turner) has a porte-cochère approached by wide steps which are flanked by balustrades. The windows carry semi-circular heads and above those facing the gates is a roundal displaying the Mulholland family emblem – an escallop shell. String course, quoins, overhanging eaves and an ashlar chimney with plinth complete this delightful little lodge.

The disused driveway from the Bangor Gate served Craigowen (demolished 1995) (Q.V.) on the sea cliff as well as Craigavad House.

When the Holywood to Bangor railway line was constructed over the parklands of the seaboard mansions (1865) the avenues were carried over the permanent way by elegant sandstone arches. In the case of the Craigowen and Craigavad House railway arch serving the drive form the Bangor Gate construction was lengthened to make provision for wide verge lawns on either side.

Today the entrance to Craigavad House is from Station Road beside the old railway halt. Once it was one of the most important stations of the Bangor line with post office, residence, waiting rooms, goods siding and crossings for the "Motor Train". The facilities closed in 1957 although they reopened for a short time in the 1960's.

XV CRAIGDARRAGH (1850) P.D.L. ST. COLUMBANUS HOUSE
CRAIGDARRAGH ROAD, BT19 1UB

Craigdarragh was built on an artificial eminence of the 100 feet contour line, this gave a panoramic view over Belfast Lough. Looking towards this bluff from the coastal path the mansion assumes the appearance of remote grandeur.

The famous Ulster architect, Charles Lanyon, designed the house for Francis Gordon Esq., who never resided there as it was tenanted for many years. Thomas Workman Esq. purchased the property about 1870; the family lived there until 1957 when it was acquired by Church Authorities to provide a residential home for senior citizens in 1959.

The Workman family was among the four world famous shipbuilders of Belfast. Sir Edward Harland (1831-1895), who in 1854 had been appointed manager of Robert Hickson's shipyard on Queen's Island, purchased the Hickson Company in 1858. Gustav W. Wolff (1834-1913), became Harland's partner in 1861. Sir George Clark (1861-1935) was a former apprentice at Harland and Wolff's Company. Francis Workman (1856-1927) established a shipyard on the River Lagan in 1877, which Sir George Clark joined in 1880. In the first years of the twentieth century the two shipyards captured ten per cent of United Kingdom production and six per cent of world output, which included Titanic, Olympic and Britannic.

Our survey of family homes which have been demolished or altered extends eastward along the south coast of Belfast Lough from Richmond to Craigdarragh, two mansions which epitomise the identity of the merchant princes who gave to the Holywood area its special ambience. Craigdarragh life-style in the early years of last century is captured charmingly by Margaret Workman, who grew up in the house before her marriage to Colonel Harry Garner.

The huge stone and stucco mansion was a fine example of the Italianate palazzo style of the Lanyon office. A deep cornice with modillion brackets surrounds the hipped roof which is emphasised by a wide frieze. The many square paned tall windows carry highly decorated mouldings, under panels and bracketed cills. The elaborate pillared porch carries

Gate Lodge

archivolts and a heavy balustrade. Above the porch is a tripartite window with panels and pilasters. The quoins are vermiculated; the chimney stacks have bracketed cornices and accommodate some thirty flues.

On the east side of the house there was an extensive stable, court-yard and farm-yard with abundant service accommodation. Beneath the house there is an extensive semi-basement and beneath the roof full attic quarters for the staff. Interior opulence is continued in the square central hall, the grand reception rooms and the quality of the woodwork and stucco work.

Laynon's client, Francis Gordon did not build a porter's lodge or entrance gates on the public road. It seems about the year 1870 Thomas Workman erected the lodge, which today is halfway down the avenue. The design is Victorian Picturesque with steeply pictched gables, a canted bay window, a gabled hallway and fretted barge-boards with hipknobs. It is extant but defaced. Ordnance Survey maps suggest formerly the modern Seahill Road continued past this lodge to link with Coastguard Avenue.

Like other properties in Church care, Craigdarragh is carefully preserved and it is our best domestic example of the work of Ulster's leading architect, Sir Charles Lanyon. Unfortunately St. Columbanus Residential Home closed in 2002.

XVI CRAIGTARA (1896) P.D.L. MY LADY'S MILE BT18 9EW

Craigtara was one of the first villas to be erected on Alexandra Avenue, the name recorded for My Lady's Mile on maps of the 1917 sale of the town. The one acre site came under complicated Lot 111, which included the grounds of the Firs, Benthorpe, Laurel Bank, Ardeen, St. Colmcilles Church and the gardens behind Walmer Terrace.

The bidding for Lot 111 in the Royal Avenue property salesrooms of Messrs. R.J. McConnell in December 1917 must have been fast and furious!

In 1917 the nominated tenant of Craigtara was Mrs G.G. Henderson, under the lease granted to her husband on 9 May 1895 for £10 per annum.

In the early years of the nineteenth century the Shepherd's Path, the original name for *"The Mile,"* led from the High Street towards the Irish Hill. Where the lane crossed the present day Demesne Road (c 1870), the Coogan Family ran a Dairy Farm. Holywood Brick Works operated from the clay beds where Norwood Lane is today.

As well as the Hendersons, others to build *"Out on the Mile"* were the Birch and Gaussen families. The Birch clan sponsored every athletic exploit in the town. J.P. was playing cricket at Rockport in his eighties! They removed to Demesne Road and gave their honourable name to Birch Drive.

Guy L. Birch was manager of the Belfast Hippodrome, Dr. Gaussen became one of Holywood's most respected physicians. The Burnsides, the Medleys, the McCalls, the Gillespies, and the Kearneys all chose My Lady's Mile as their environ.

Eventually the name *"Alexandra"* was reserved for the park which ran from the Mile to serve large red-brick town houses similar to Craigtara.

Craigtara's grand panelled front door was in a projecting bay with its own hip roof, on either side of which were two storey canted bay windows. The door-case arch with fanlight and paired third storey windows above bay windows carried lancet heads, all with label mouldings. Decorative terracotta lozenges, finials, string courses and roof brackets enhanced the high Victorian ambience.

The interior of Craigtara was equally ambitious. A huge reception room at the rear provided adequate space for lavish hospitality.

In the 1980's Craigtara was divided into apartments. It was demolished in the 1990's to make way for fourteen superior dwellings.

XVII CROFT COTTAGE OR THE CROFT (1868)

A.P.D.L. 2 CROFT ROAD BT18 OPB CROFT RISE

Croft Cottage was built in 1868, probably by Francis Rea who retired to Holywood from ownership of an extensive cotton manufacturing business in Belfast. No doubt this was *"One of the handsome villas of High Holywood built on land leased from J. O'Reilly Blackwood Esq. (Irish Builder).*

It was situated on the Ballymenoch side of Croft Road, then newly laid down from Ballykeel Road to Bangor Road.

The most interesting member of the Rea family was John (1822-1881). He was an eccentric solicitor whose chancery suit against Belfast Corporation led to the foundation of the Liberal Party. In 1855 his efforts assured the election of Bernard Hughes (later of Riverston House Q.V.) to Belfast Town Council. On one day of the week John Rea's contradictory conscience convinced him that Orange Tenets were correct; the following day he was an ardent Nationalist. He described himself as *"Her Orthodox Presbyterian Britannic Majesty's Orange – Fenian Attorney General of Ulster".* In his Belfast lodging the mad-cap solicitor possessed a diverse political library, busts of revolutionaries, an armoury, dogs, cats and foul-beaked parrots! Whether or not he brought any of these to the sanity of High Holywood is unknown.

J.P. Birch, born in Holywood in 1872, wrote *"John Rea was a man of magnificent physique and a brilliant lawyer who lived with his father in the Croft. He committed suicide in 1882".*

Croft Cottage was a traditional rectangular two storey villa residence. Large canted bay windows, with pilasters guarded the richly moulded door case which carried scrolled brackets, pediment and fan light. The five first storey windows connected by a wide string course, had semi-circular heads. Quoins were rather larger than usual; the eaves were carried on modillion brackets. The roof had cresting.

On the ease side of the house a battlemented wall supported an extensive conservatory with red quarry tile floor and an interesting lead spire ornamental finial. To the rear a large court yard led to stove houses. There was a huge lead water tank in the yard for domestic, equestrian and horticultural purposes, as Holywood reservoir did not materialise until 1882. Before that year houses like Croft Cottage depended upon spring wells and lead lined tanks, for the collection of rain water. Even our drinking water pipes were made from lead! How we survived lead poisoning remains a mystery! As late as the 1950's, when my family was living at Clanbrassil, the domestic water supply depended upon the vagary of a private hydraulic ram connected to a sweet spring well.

In its final years the Croft was divided into two apartments. It was demolished in 2000 and the three houses of Croft Rise were built on the site.

XVIII CROFT HOUSE (1866) A.P.D.L. 17 CROFT ROAD
CROFT MANOR BT18 OPB

Until the middle of the nineteenth century Croft Road was a lane-way leading from the Ballykeel Road at the bridge over the Croft Burn, which at that time was known as the Stinking Burn!

It seems the grounds of Croft House covered part of the Model Farm on which the few students of the County Down Agricultural College learned their trade. After its closure the fields became McKibbens' Farm which later was the home of the Ballagh Family.

In 1866 Dr. Milford Barnett, a naval surgeon, built Croft House for his retirement years. Perhaps it was at that time that the old farm lane commenced extension to the Bangor Road.

In 1867 'The Irish Builder' recorded *"A large portion of the lower part of Ballymenoch has been rented from Mr J. O'Reilly Blackwood on which very handsome villas are in the process of erection"*. This was High Holywood and one of the very handsome villas was Croft House.

In 1888 Robert Lloyd Patterson (1836-1906) came to live in Croft House. He received a knighthood in 1902 and died on 29 January 1906.

Sir Robert's grandfather was Robert Patterson, founder of the famous Patterson Hardware Emporium in Belfast (1786). Sir Robert's father was Robert Patterson (1802-1872), Fellow of the Royal Society and founder member of the Belfast Natural History Society (1821). He was president of the Society on several occasions. As an author his book 'Zoology for Schools' (1846) was *"Necessitas Scholesticorum"*.

Sir Robert's brother was William Hugh Patterson (1835-1918), a member of the Royal Irish Academy and author of *"A Glossary of Words in use in the Counties of Antrim and Down"* (1880). Sir Robert's sister was Maria Patterson (1840-1930) mother of Rosamund and Robert Lloyd Praeger, Holywood's famous siblings. The Praeger family lived in the neighbouring Woodburn House from 1868 until 1891.

Sir Robert was educated at the Royal Academical Institution and after school days he was apprenticed to the Linen Trade. He was elected President of the Belfast Chamber of Trade and of the Natural History and Philosophical Society. His book *"Birds, Fishes and Cetacea of Belfast Lough"* shows where his leisure time interests lay – like all the other members of this multi-talented Holywood family!

Sir Robert Lloyd Patterson died at Croft House on 29 January 1906. Some time afterwards the Cook family lived there in considerable style. They were one of the few families in the area who possessed a motorcar and a chauffeur. Little Miss Cook (a delightful Holywood resident for many years) was widely envied when driven to and from the many children's parties of those far off days, the rest of us were perambulatory!

The big house was acquired by the Department of Health & Social Services and refurbished as an excellent residence for senior citizens. Much to the regret of the people of Holywood, Croft House was demolished, although still in pristine condition. In the early 1990's New Croft House was opened in the grounds of Marmion (Q.V.) on Church Road.

And so disappeared one of High Holywood's finest villa residences. Five bays on the west façade looked down over the Croft Burn to catch the afternoon sunshine. A full semi-elliptical bay window rose through both stories on the

Croft House

Woodburn House

north or entrance front which carried 3 more bays and a large balustraded porch. The attic floor was illuminated by dormers set into the hipped roof. Windows on the ground floor had semi-circular heads, elaborate mouldings, bracketed cills and drip-courses. First storey windows were similar, but with concave heads. All openings were crowned with pronounced key stones. The interior of the house was mid-Victorian artisanship at its very best and remained in that condition until its unfortunate destruction.

The site was used for the construction of the seven dwellings known as Croft Manor.

IXX CROFTON HALL (C1867) BANGOR ROAD, BT18 ONE

Crofton Hall was one of the group of villas built in High Holywood after the alignment of Croft Road from Ballykeel Road to Bangor Road. The Irish Builder (1867) refers to the development as *"very handsome villas on land rented from Mr J O'Reilly Blackwood"*.

Other houses in the group are Croft Cottage (Q.V.) Croft House (Q.V.) Salernum, Beechcroft Manse (Q.V.) Woodburn House and Hill Croft.

Crofton Hall was build by William Moreland in 1867, a director of the prosperous Loopbridge Flax Spinning Company.

The stuccoed entrance façade overlooked Seapark and the lough. A pair of gabled roofs were connected by an inset bay which on the ground floor extended into a large porch. The entrance porch was flanked by two canted bay windows, all were capped with cornices.

Above the bay windows were tripartites with label mouldings. Generally the quoins were unobtrusive except for those beside the panelled double front doors, which were Irish pilasters. Cills were bracketed. Features of the house were the extended eaves and waved bargeboards rising from carved pendent toes to tall hipknobs with spiky finials.

On the west side of the house a conservatory had been attached to a battlemented wall which concealed the yard with its adequate domestic accommodation.

A pretty little gate lodge in the same style as the house graced the fanciful Tudor Gothic gate piers on the Bangor Road. It was one and a half storey, three bay symmetrical and gabled and built on a cellar or basement floor. The semi-circular headed windows were arranged in pairs with label mouldings; that to the central recessed porch of the entrance front formed a pendant dripstone. As with the big house the chimney stacks had moulded cornice cappings and octagonal yellow terracotta pots.

The gatelodge was demolished in 1970 to facilitate road works. The house lasted for an additional two decades and then was demolished to make way for the three dwellings of Crofton Glen and two houses on Croft Road.

XX CULLODEN (1876) P.D.L. 140 BANGOR ROAD BT18 OEY
CULLODEN HOTEL

Culloden Moor near Inverness was the site of the battle between the Young Pretender (Charles Edward Stuart) and the butcher (Duke of Cumberland) which terminated the Jacobite Rising (1745). The Duke received a pension, the flower "Sweet William" took his name and G.F. Handel composed an oratorio in his honour! The Pretender fled to the continent. Bagpipes were banned, the wearing of kilts was frowned open and Scotland came under one jurisdiction to establish peace, order and good government.

The battle may have influenced W.A. Robinson, in his choice of a name for his grand Irish house. As Robinson was a Scotsman, a more probable reason was that the family name of his wife, Elizabeth Jane, was Culloden.

William Auchinleck Robinson, a Scottish stock broker came to Belfast in the 1850; for some years he lived on the Antrim Road. Mr and Mrs Robinson removed to Cultra and lived in a cottage on the future Culloden estate, while the new house was being built to the design of Messrs Young and MacKenzie (1876).

The house was constructed in squared quarry-faced sandstone smoothly dressed and transported to Cultra from the Scottish quarries via Portaferry harbour.

The mansion is dominated by a crenellated central tower with corbelled bartizan, string cources and balconette over the deep chaimfered and pillared doors' case. These details are continued in the bulstraded bay windows and a delightful little second storey circular corbelled bay window to the right of the tower. The tall chimneys are set diagonally on plinths.

Interior stucco work, the central hall and receptions rooms remain in the original condition. The fine stained glass window lighting the grand staircase and the proprietary chapel were added when the house became an ecclesiastical palace.

Between the house and Bangor road a walled kitchen garden and an elaborate stable court-yard were constructed in the Scottish baronial style of the entire complex. A fountain played into a circular bowl to the south of the front doors and a private gate opened unto Cultra railway station.

There is a gatelodge of the same date as the house and constructed in the same style with quarry-faced sandstone. It is one and a half storey having a steeply pitched roof with shamrock finials. The cottage has a canted bay window surmounted by a dormer with a shouldered window opening. It has a gabled porch with lancet arch.

After W.A. Robinson died in 1884, Mrs Robinson conveyed the house to the Church of Ireland for use as a palace for the Bishop of Down, Conor and Dromore. The chaste Robinson mausoleum is in the priory graveyard. The beautiful west window in the Parish Church, where W.A. Robinson was a vestryman, is a memorial to Elizabeth Jane Robinson.

Bishop Welland (1892-1907) removed from Ardtullagh to the new palace in 1899. Bishop Crozier lived at Cultra from 1907 to 1911, when he was elected Archbishop of Armagh. Bishop D'Arcy enjoyed the palace before his transfer to Dublin in 1919. Bishop Grierson resided at Culloden Palace for a few months, then removed to the See House on Antrim Road in 1920.

In 1923 Culloden House was bought by Sir John Campbell, gynaecologist of Royal Victoria Hospital. The Campbell family removed to the Malone Road in 1956 and Culloden was bought by the proprietors of White's Milk Bars Ltd., who refurbished the house as a first-class hotel.

The hotel was acquired by the Hasting's Hotel Group Ltd. The building was sympathetically extended with several wings and the impressive Elysium Leisure Facility. The Cultra Inn was built in the extensive hotel gardens. Today the complete campus presents Ulster's leading five star hotel.

Messrs. Fairbrother and Clark of London Donegall Arms, Belfast. Tuesday, 25th October, 1854

Under Order of the High Court of Chancery made in the case of Higgins v Earl of Shaftesbury and Others

The whole of the rising town of Holywood Numerous private residences, shops, hotels, parcels of land and building ground.

The Holywood Demesne, most of Knocknagoney, Priory Park, The Kinnegar and Woodlands.

Gentlemen's residences – Ashfield (the Bishop's Palace), Westbrook, Clifton House, Maryfield, Richmond House, Knocknagoney House, in all about 1,500 acres producing a gross rental of £1,600.

Particularly valuable to capitalists and building speculators from its contiguity to the Port of Belfast and Railway communication thereto.

Holywood is a pleasing and healthy resort, the favourite and most fashionable bathing place on Belfast Lough and the resort of the Residents of Belfast.

IN THE HIGH COURT OF JUSTICE IN IRELAND – CHANCERY DIVISION – LAND JUDGES

TOWN AND LANDS OF HOLYWOOD, PRIORY PARK AND KNOCKNAGONEY

BARONY OF CASTLEREAGH LOWER AND COUNTY DOWN VALUABLE FEE-FARM AND OTHER HEAD RENTS AND BUILDING SITES

TO BE SOLD BY PUBLIC AUSTION IN 117 LOTS BY MESSRS R J McCONNELL & CO, AT THEIR PROPERTY SALE ROOMS

ON TUESDAY, THE 4th DAY OF DECEMBER, 1917 AND FOLLOWING DAYS

COMMENCING EACH DAY AT TWELVE O'CLOCK NOON

BY DIRECTION OF THE RIGHT HONOURABLE MR JUSTICE ROSS

XXI CULTRA HOUSE C1672 (P.D.L. CULTRA HOUSE BT18 OCT)

In the year 1671 John Kennedy acquired the townlands *"Ballyrobert, Balleydavey, Craig-a-Vad, Ballygrainy, Ballycaltre, Corrow Reagh and Ballybun"*. (Mason's statistical survey 1819). These townlands had been part of the Hamilton estates before the sale by Lord Clanbrassil. About that time Cultra House was built in the most advantageous and beautiful part of the new 4000 acre Kennedy Estate.

Rev. W.A. Holmes, installed Vicar of Holywood in 1810, described the mansion house *"as an old structure, but the present proprietor is now adding to and improving it after the Gothic fashion. The tasteful display of planting and the natural advantages of the situation render this a very beautiful place"*.

During the improvement, parts of the original mansion were refurbished, a battlemented parapet was added and label mouldings put over windows and doors. In 1832 a view of the refurbished house was drawn by Joseph Molloy, engraved by E.K. Proctor and published by Morgan Jetlett of Belfast.

In 1850 Thomas Kelly the local surgeon described the house *"a mansion of great antiquity, built upwards of two hundred years ago, and still a building of considerable extent and of some architectural pretensions. The Demesne occupies nearly three hundred acres in extent, thickly wooded, arranged in the taste of the 17th Century. Few situation can be more imposing or romantic than Cultra. In different parts it is over-shadowed by numerous luxuriant oak trees of singularly beautiful form and growth. The gigantic size attained by some is surprising and their long graceful branches reaching to the ground, produce an effect not unlike that we have heard, of the Banyan Groves in the Plains of India. Several rare wild plants, important in botanical science, also decorate the Demesne"*.

It seems the pleasure gardens of the big house were open to the public for recreation. A fuller account of the Kennedys of Cultra is recorded in the companion volume *"Holywood, Then and Now"*. Suffice it to mention here the more illustrious members of the Kennedy Family. John, a magistrate, was a supporter of the United Irishman (1798). Sir Arthur was Governor of Western Australia, British Columbia, Hong Kong and Queensland (d. 1883). Sir Robert was an outstandingly successful member of the Diplomatic Service. The Hon. Lady Bertha, daughter of Viscount Bangor, was an Edwardian adventures, friend of Queen Victoria and Embassy wife extraordinaire.

Present day Cultra Avenue follows the route of the carriage driveway to the big house, then continues to the harbour. A cruciform gate lodge was built opposite the entrance gates on Bangor Road. On the west side of the avenue there was vast kitchen and market walled garden with accommodation for the outdoor staff.

A pictorial map (c. 1865) shows the north façade of the large rambling building. The main house has three parallel gabled roofs, the first and second of which have three storey bays beneath and show double windows and attics. The third bay carries a very large two storey canted bay window. There is a west facing two storey 'T' shaped wing which has four bays. The pictorial map is entitled *"Houses to be let at Cultra, Co. Down"*. Among these is *"Cultra House – A Large Mansion on 5 acres of ground"*.

Anecdotally the family rented out the big house in the latter years of the nineteenth century and used Mayfield Cottage (17, Seafront Road, BT18 OBB) as *"pied-à-terre"*.

Several families enjoyed life-style in Cultra House and various alterations were made.

When Sir Robert and Lady Kennedy retired from the Diplomatic Service at the end of the century, they built a grand new house, Cultra Manor (Bangor Road, BT18 OEU) and removed there after 1902.

Cultra House continued to be a comfortable family home until the 1970's, then the McCormick family donated it *"for the benefit of the people of Holywood"*. Another one of their many gifts to Holywood was Johnny the Jig Playground.

So after two centuries Cultra House became a hospital for those with mental difficulties. When it outlived this function the Holywood people looked forward to removal of its ancient parts to the Manor Museum. However, in the event the Government Department concerned sold the valuable land for building development. Fortunately the house was acquired by a family which values our heritage. It has been restored to its nineteenth century magnificence.

The lands around the old house provided building sites for eleven residences; the carriage driveway became Cultra Park.

Edwardian classical Cultra Manor was the last mansion house built on the North Down shore line. The grounds of Sorrento (Q.V.) and Dalcoolin (Q.V.) were added to the Manor Park. Today this is the campus of the Ulster Folk and Transport Museum.

Cultra House

XXII DALCHOOLIN (C.1825) A.P.D.L. ULSTER TRANSPORT MUSEUM
BANGOR ROAD BT18 OBY

Wellington Lodge was built about the year 1825 by William Crawford, agent of Hugh Kennedy, proprietor of the extensive Cultra Estate. William Crawford was a solicitor with a lucrative law practise in Belfast and Dublin. The sagacious agent bought from his employer the lands around Wellington in 1847. The park extended from the shores of Belfast Lough to the Holywood and Bangor main road.

In 1850 Surgeon Kelly described Wellington as a modern family residence possessing high architectural pretensions. *"Wellington is the residence of William Crawford, solicitor. It is built according to the Elizabethan style of Architecture. The beautiful gardens which surround it exhibit the highest skill in horticulture; and the tasteful hand of the florist has not been wanting in the arrangement of the rare and beautiful flora which decorate these grounds"*. In 1867 the house, now called Dalchoolin, was purchased by James Moore Esq., J.P. It seems the new owner completely refurbished the building to produce a Tudor revival pile with pinnacled gables, turrets and barley sugar chimney pots.

In 1896 Dalchoolin became the property of Edwin Hughes, J.P., another prosperous Belfast solicitor. Soon the estate became famous for equestrian prowess and fine stable accommodation, which was approached through a distinctive arched gateway.

A walled kitchen garden and elaborate fountain lay to the east of the stable yard. To the west of the mansion the main carriage avenue, which led to the main road, continued down the hill to a slip-way on the lough shore. Here another high archway guarded the seagate with its adjacent estate cottages.

A third driveway led from the house to Circular Road East at the gates of which stands the only extant lodge. In latter days this became the main approach to the mansion and stables. A delightful little lodge in the extravagant Tudor revival style of the main house protected the Bangor Road gates. Today a car park covers the site of the cottage.

In 1970 Dalchoolin was acquired by the trustees of the Ulster Folk Museum. The campus is opposite the gates to Cultra Manor Museum Headquarters. Proximity to the railway lines made Dalchoolin an ideal site for a Transport Museum. Cultra station was brought back into service and a branch railway line extended unto the site.

By the early 1970's the mansion had been allowed to deteriorate. It was demolished, the sea arch and cottages were removed about the same time. The lands facing Circular Road East were used for executive style housing.

Gate Lodge

Dalcoolin entrance front

XXIII EASDALE (C.1860) A.P.D.L. 28 VICTORIA ROAD, BT18 9BD

Formerly Esdale was called Donneybrook; the name was altered before the publication of the 1937 Ordnance Survey map.

The extensive grounds ran from Victoria Road to the Croft Burn and from Hillbrook (Q.V. Number 24) to Number 42. To the south of the House was a small artificial motte, presumably created for decorative purposes. Adequate stabling and horticultural offices were established close to the Croft Burn.

The north façade of the house had the appearance of an original entrance front with several irregular bays. It was sited to the east of Hillbrook (Q.V.) affording a lough view before afforestation and building construction obscured the vista.

About 1900 the south façade was sympathetically refurbished to become the entrance front. On either side of a roofed porch large circular two storey extensions were added to the corners of the original building, each had four windows to both floors. Windows on this side of the house were modern three pane casements; those to the rest of the building were traditional four rectangular pane sash. A domestic wing extended towards the Croft Burn.

The main house was square with a hipped roof carried on ornamental brackets. A huge multi-flued central chimney stack with terracotta pots dominated the house. String courses and roof brackets were successfully carried into the 1900 refurbishment.

The grand old house was divided into three commodious apartments before demolition in 1997 to accommodate an additional four new houses to the couple already on the site and a house to be called Glendale on Victoria Road.

Easdale was the fifth fine Victorian mansion of the High Holywood group to be needlessly demolished to provide building sites. About forty houses of the group remain, including two majestic terraces. It is imperative that the town realises the importance of the unique collection of Victorian homes and the important part it plays in our heritage. We should assert High Holywood to be an area of special townscape character.

XXIV ELDON XXIV HOUSE (C.1860) A.P.D.L. KINNEGAR (ARMY PROPERTY) BT18 9JR

Eldon House was erected on the Kinnegar lough shore in the 1860's, that was before the advent of Ireland's first Golf Club (Kinnegar 1881); the Holywood Cricket and Lawn Tennis Club (Kinnegar 1879) and the Ulster Rifle Club (Kinnegar 1870).

John Power, (1797 – 1874) selected a remote point of the old Cunifar Peninsula for his new house. John Power was proprietor of the Belfast Hotel, Holywood's leading hostelry. He was a town commissioner with many other business interests in Holywood. He married into the well-known Ballagh family.

The best known member of the family was Sir. John Cecil Power (1870 – 1950), Member of Parliament for Wimbledon, founder member of the Institute of Historical Research and the Royal Humane Society.

Eldon House became the property of Robert Erskine Esq., who as founder member of the Cricket and Lawn Tennis Club allowed the players to use the building at the rear of Eldon House as a pavilion. Army use of the Kinnegar for summer camping experience commenced in 1885. In 1887 the War Office acquired a portion of the lands and bought "Ashfield", the Bishop's palace, on the south-side of the railway line. Eventually the government obtained the entire curtilage beyond Kinnegar Drive, after which Eldon House was used as the official residence of the Range Warden. Later the old house was added to the long list of Holywood houses which the Army demolished by explosion. (Ashfield, Westbrook, Holywood House, Oakley, Eldon, Golf Villas, and Laburnum Cottage).

A photograph subscribed *"Kinnegar Holywood, Co. Down 1881, birth place of the Royal Belfast Golf Club"* shows the founder members in front of Eldon House. The group includes Sir G. Clark, Sir D. Dixon, Dr. W.F. Collier, J.G. McGee, A N Charley, H M Charley, W.H. Philips, C. Topping, W.E. Williams and many other Holywood worthies.

The sea front façade of Eldon House was dominated by a huge double storey bay window. It carried a balconette and commanded the view which Surgeon Kelly described *"not inferior to the shores of the Mediterranean, Carrickfergus Bay, the Black Mountain, Cavehill, the Carnmoney Mountains, the town and romantic Castle of Carrickfergus, terminating with the Basaltic Columns of Black-Head"*.

Eldon House had wide eaves with wide cornice and modillion brackets. Several string courses surrounded the building; its quoins were described as Irish pilaster.

The carriage driveway ran by the lough shore and arrived at Kinnegar Drive beyond "Golf Villas". Golf Villas was a pair of semi-detached residences. Soon the house beside the home green was used as a club house, if not that house then a wooden chalet in its rear garden served the purpose.

XXV ESPLANADE COTTAGE (C.1850) P.D.L. 1, THE ESPLANADE BT18 9JG

Lot 28 in the 1917 sale comprised some ten acres of Kinnegar land between the railway line and the Esplanade; the Esplanade itself being retained by the owner as a roadway and not acquired by the Urban Council.

Mrs Elizabeth Hunter was tenant of the entire Lot 28, except for item 91, a triangle of 12 perches beside the gates to the railway station; this was Esplanade Cottage. Mrs Hunter's lease was dated 29 January 1858, John Harrison to William Weatherall. The separate lease of the little cottage was dated 14 December 1868 to James Pink for £3 per annum subject to the covenants *"not to build or permit the building of any house or houses at any time on side premises and not to assign or sub-let any part thereof without the previous consent of the lessor"*.

In 1848 the original Charles Lanyon designed railway station terminated the line at Marine Parade. Today the Throughpass runs over part of the site. In 1854 construction work commenced to continue the rail service to Bangor. A second terminus was erected for the Bangor line – a couple of meters higher that the platform for the train to Belfast. The new line ran on an embankment which bisected the Marine Parade. This created the odd triangle of land on which Esplanade Cottage stood. The Esplanade was built on reclaimed land on the seaside of the embankment to the point where track elevation allowed an underpass for Kinnegar traffic.

A photograph taken by W.A. Green in 1920 shows the cottage, and the Esplanade crowded with spectators during the Sailing Club Regetta of that year.

It commanded a splendid view of the lough and the County Antrim coast. A garden stretched into the top of the triangle. The walls of the sloping approach to the 'down' platform of the Belfast and County Down Railway Co. ran along the back of the property.

The cottage was built in red brick, possibly the product of the Holywood brick works on the Shepherd's Path. It had three bays, the windows were doubled and as with the door case all were lancet arched. The roof rafters were exposed beneath the guttering. Accommodation in the little cottage provided a hallway, four rooms, all with fireplaces and a scullery in a single extension at the rear. The water closet and rubbish pit were situated in the corner of the triangular garden.

In the 1930's the charming little seaside cottage was demolished and semi-detached houses built on the vacant site.

Before we leave the Kinnegar and travel along the coast to Glencraig at Craigavad, let us take a brief look at a few Kinnegar memories.

"Holywood Then and Now" records how Charles McCadden (1842-1912), who hailed from Rathmullan, bought the Kinnegar Hotel and other properties on Park Road and Milton Street from Daniel Shipp in 1874. A map which accompanied the sale calls the Esplanade "Park Road" and Kinnegar Road "Milton Street". By 1917 Bryron Street had emerged over a right of way which ran behind the old Music Hall. To remind himself of Donegal, Charles McCadden built "Rathmullan" and "Buncrana" on the Kinnegar.

Walking westward along the Esplanade, Ivy place was on the left, then Kinnegar Hotel, Seaview Terrace, Kinnegar Villa, Villa Nova and Anchor Lodge, all of which had uninterrupted views over the lough.

Pierview Cottage, Pierview Terrace, St. Leonard's (formerly Milton Park) and Prospect Terrace were built on Kinnegar Road, formerly they had splendid sea views.

Byron Place, the Gas Works, Gloucester Terrace and Marine Place were situated on Byron Street (now called Kinnegar Drive).

XXVI GLENCRAIG (1833) P.D.L. SEAHILL ROAD BT18 0DA

G Scott, one of the civil assistants working on the Ordnance Survey (1834) claimed *"Glencarrick in the townland of Ballyrobert is the residence of Miss Sims"*. Miss Mary Symes commenced construction during the previous year. Surgeon Kelly included the new house among the commodious summer residences situated at Rockport.

Miss Symes; a generous donor to all Holywood charities, lived in Glencraig until her death in 1863. This good lady donated the site for Glencraig Parish Church at the gates of her thirty-one acres of seaboard Park Lands. The lease was dated 10 October 1856 *"setting apart free from all rent for Glencraig Church, in which the Litany and Rites of the United Church of England and Ireland as by law established, shall be used and observed"*.

About the year 1840 a gate lodge was erected at the grand entrance. It was a three bay symmetrical cottage with label moulded openings. Its walls were stuccoed and had quoins.

The well known Craigavon family took up residence at Glencraig in 1923, shortly after the formation of the Stormont Government (June 1921) of which Sir James Craig was Prime Minister.

By the war years (1944) the Swains, followed by the Nobles were training horses on the green acres of Glencraig. After the death of William Noble in 1950 (Nobel and Company Ltd. Bag and Sack manufacturers), Glencraig was acquired by the Hospitals Authority and two years later was transferred to the Royal Victoria Hospital.

On 18 September 1954 the Dowager Marchioness of Londonderry opened Glencraig Curative School. Shortly afterwards the neighbouring Craigowen House, on the shore cliff was added to Glencraig Camphill Community Campus. Today the campus covers one hundred acres. There are nineteen houses; schools, workshops, a village centre and a working farm at the heart of the two hundred strong community population.

Glencraig was built in the Tudor revival style of architecture with many pinnacles and gables. The walls were crenellated and the gables surmounted with shafts and finials. Camphill Community refurbished the house in 1993. Today it is one of the best examples of early Victorian architecture in the area.

Craigowen now demolished, was a "T"–shaped mansion with a central court yard, built on the sea cliff in the second half of the nineteenth century. It sported an elaborate parapet, quoins, a large porch and unusual diagonally set sandstone chimney stacks on square bases. Old Craigowen was demolished in 1995 and a new building erected in its place.

In its heyday Craigowen shared the fine Bangor gate lodge of Craigavad House (Q.V.)

Glencraig House

XXVII GRAY'S BUILDINGS
(1830'S) P.D.L. MARINE PARADE SOUTH ENTRY TO SUBWAY UNDER THROUGH PASS BT18 9HZ

About the year 1830 John Gray started to build a terrace of four town houses on the Marine Parade, the work was completed by 1835. A lease was granted to John Gray by Dorothea Kennedy from 1 November 1835 at a rent of sixteen pounds for one rood and twenty perches of Holywood sea front land..

The House of Industry (1813) rather eclipsed the site of the west end residence; it was built at an oblique angle viewing the sandy coastline towards Clanbrassil. Marine Cottage occupied the site at the east end of the terrace.

John Gray built his terrace eighteen years before the Holywood to Belfast railway terminus was built, and thirty five years before the embankment which extended the railway line to Bangor ,materialised. The 1860 earth works bisected the Marine Parade directly in front of Gray's buildings.

Both Ordnance Survey maps of 1834 and 1858 show the Terrace; strangely neither of the maps indicate sea defences along Marine Parade.

In his *"History of Holywood"* (1850) Surgeon Kelly records *"On the West Side stands Marine Parade which commences at the Terminus of the Railway Station and faces the Sea. Here are situate a beautiful row of houses called Gray'sBbuildings, which, in point of internal comfort and architectural completeness can vie with any"*. High praise indeed!

George Craik, Professor of English Literature and History at the Queen's College chose the terrace by the sea, at his home. Colleague Professor John Ferrie emulated Craik's good example, as did Doctor Blain. The well known Munce family, who contributed much to the wellbeing of Holywood lived there for many years, and Captain John Auld brought his bride, my mother, there in the 1930's. That particular angled house, where I spent the first year of life, was demolished in the 1970's for the construction of the Holywood Throughpass. The other houses in the terrace lived on until the 1990's when they followed the fate of so many of our historic buildings.

Gray's Buildings

XXVIII   HILL BROOK (1852) P.D.L. 22 & 24 VICTORIA ROAD BT18 9BG

In 1852 William Bankhead Esq., commissioned Architect Thomas Turner to design a mansion, out buildings and porters lodge for a High Holywood site. Turner had served his apprenticeship under the famous Charles Lanyon and branched out on his own account in 1851, after a brief practice in Scotland.

One day Turner called at the site when he was on his way to supervise building operations at Craigavad House (Q.V.), where a fine neo-classical mansion was being built for John Mulholland. Correspondence dated 1854 to Mr Bankhead, refers to this visit and invites payment of the Holywood accounts! Perhaps default was the reason why the porter's lodge never saw the light of day. The house was completed but certain areas show greater attention to detail than others! The house was divided into a pair of semi-detached villas, after minimal re-planning, and has remained so into the new millennium.

In the 1850's part of the building was used as one of the High Holywood schools, under the strict tutelage of schoolmaster John Turpin. One document claims Hillbrook school operated in the neighbouring residence "Glenburn". The proliferation of schools in High Holywood at that time, suggests both houses may have been used for educational purposes (See "Holywood Then and Now"). From 1858 to 1869 William Robertson Esq., J.P. of Messrs Robertson, Ledlie, Ferguson and Company lived in Hillbrook. The firm's headquarters in Belfast, with branches in Cork and Waterford, had world acknowledgement and the patronage of Queen Victoria. Established in 1853 at the Castle Tramway Junction on the former site of the Northern Banking Company, the Bank Buildings provided retail shopping accommodation and manufacturing capacity. Fashionable architect W.H. Lynn designed the huge edifice, which at that time was one of the largest in the United Kingdom. A speciality of the firm was the production of Columkille Damask linen, into which was woven elaborate designs from the Book of Kells. In 1979 the Bank Buildings became Belfast Primark.

A second Holywood entrepreneur, who resided at Hillbrook until his death in 1955, was Claud Henfrey, the ice-cream manufacturer who introduced choc-ices to Ireland. His collection of early photographs is a worthy contribution to Holywood history. Another resident was Dick Rogers, author and early ecologist.

In 1888 the Ladies Branch of the Royal Belfast Golf Club was founded at a meeting in Hillbrook when it was the home of Mrs R. Young. Mrs Young became the club's first treasurer. The family of another committee member, Mrs Kemp, lived in Hillbrook for many years.

Today the semi-detached residences are meticulously maintained by the Addis and Coulter families.

XXIX HOLYWOOD HOUSE (C.1706) A.P.D.L. ABBEY PLACE BT18 9PR

Surgeon Kelly (1850) recorded *"Holywood House is an extensive building situated a few perches south of the town. The face of the mansion has an antique air calculated to impress the stranger with the belief that several centuries have passed over it. But it is not so – its builder was Simon Isaac Esq., the late proprietor of Holywood estate. The extensive grounds which surround it were formally well wooded and gave to it all the external characteristics of an aristocratic abode. The present occupant is John Thompson Esq., J.P."*. The following year Henry Harrison was in residence.

Simon Isaac was land agent to Hans Hamilton, grandson of Sir Hans Hamilton who had inherited Holywood from his cousin the Earl Clanbrassil. Young Hans was forced to offer for sale the debt encumbered estate (in Newtownards, 1705) – the highest bidder was his land agent! Shortly afterwards Simon Isaac erected the mansion house.

The house featured in the 1740 survey (Harris and Smith); maps of County Down (1767 and 1810); Miss Tate's map of Belfast Lough (1775); Statistical Account of Ireland (1819); Records for the first Ordnance Survey of Ireland (1834) and all Ordnance Survey maps up to the Second World War. In his note for the Statistical Survey (1819) Rev. W.A. Holmes recorded *"Holywood House was built by Simon Isaac Esq., then proprietor of the Holywood Estate, a gentleman whose memory is much revered by the inhabitants. The external appearance of this mansion is formal and old fashioned, but great attention and expense have been bestowed on it. It is at present the property of William Kennedy Esq., now resident in the East Indies, by whom the estate has been lately purchased. It is about four miles distant from Belfast, South Side".*

In 1796 the grandson of Simon Isaac bequeathed the estate to his nephew, Thomas Bunburry (who respectfully took the Isaac name). His son Simon, sold the estate to William Kennedy of Bombay in the East Indies. (12 December 1812).

Mrs Dorothea Kennedy (William's widow) bequeathed the estate to charity; her irate daughter contested the Will and the estate was sold to John Harrison Esq., of neighbouring Mertoun Hall (Q.V.) (24 October 1854). John Harrison's son Henry, already a tenant in Holywood House since 1851, continued to live there until his death in 1873, the same year in which his daughter, Margaret, married Colonel John McCance of the nearby Knockgoney House (Q.V.).

Holywood House was not included in the sale of the Harrison estates in Belfast on 4 December 1917. In the following years various tenants inhabited the mansion, the best known residents were members of the Lough family. The Loughs supplied thirsty Holywood town with grade 'A' milk and cream from their prize winning tuberculin-tested dairy herd.

In the 1930's the Governors of Sullivan Upper School acquired the lands to the east of the front carriage driveway of Holywood House, for use as sports fields. In 1938 the Governors decided to remove the school from the town centre to the green field site on which Sullivan Upper School had flourished ever since.

During the Second World War, the War Department vested the lands to the west side of the Avenue for use as a prisoner of war encampment. The Army considered the structure of Holywood House unsafe and demolished it in

1941. The mansion had withstood the test of time for almost a quarter of a millennium, it disappeared in a day! Now all that remains of the campus are the walls of the orchard and kitchen gardens.

As I remember it, Holywood House was a very plain large Georgian redbrick pile. Shallow steps led up to a wide sandstone flagged patio which, like the steps, extended the full length of the mansion.

The house contained two main floors; above which extended a maze of attic rooms, below stairs stretched a labyrinth of dark, damp culinary and servants apartments, wine cellars and curving passages. Other bricklined passages led beyond the perimeter of the house. Over the years the tunnels have acquired traditional tales of local adventure. The passages which extended towards the lough shore were sewage conduits; a large underground chamber, which ran in the opposite direction may have been the mansion's ice-house. Two vast return wings extended into the rear courtyard. The terminal of the east wing encompassed the mansion's back lodge. This guarded the high gates which opened into the courtyard. The much-used back entrance into the house was situated in the east wing.

The court yard extended beyond the west wing into the farm yard. It was surrounded by two storeyed stone agricultural buildings. Additional estate workers' cottages and a traditional 'cowstail' Irish pump completed the extensive quadrangle. The back drive let to the old Holywood Road junction; the Nun's Walk continued over Demesne Road into the yard.

Rev. James O'Laverty, P.P. thought a conventual establishment stood in the vicinity of Holywood House. He based the possibility on marbles inscribed with a cross and Latin text, which were found in the gardens.

At the Belfast Road terminal of the main entrance driveway (now Abbey ring) a pretty gate lodge guarded the main entrance. It remained longer than the mansion house. Today the site is lawn covered and the tree which shaded the little cottage is extant.

The story of the Harrison family is recorded in the companion volume *"Holywood Then and Now"*.

XXX THE HOUSE OF INDUSTRY (C. 1813) A.P.D.L. THROUGH PASS AT SOUTH ENTRANCE TO SUB-WAY BT18 9HZ

In 1824 a House of Commons Committee recommended a town-land survey of Ireland with maps at the scale of six inches to the mile. Prime Minister, the Duke of Wellington, himself an Irishman, authorized this first Ordnance Survey. It was undertaken by Royal Engineers and a party of civil cartographers.

Lieutenants G.F.W. Bordes made his statistical report on the parish of Holywood on 29 September 1834. On the following 7 October Lieutenant T.A. Larcom wrote to his colleague: *"My dear Bordes, Holywood is a very nice memoir …. It would be very desirable to give some more account of the poor house, because they are very unusual in Ireland"*. Archibald McLachlan supplied the relevant information on 1 December 1834. *"Poor Houses: These poor houses were originally work houses or houses of industry. People quite destitute are taken into the poor house and if they can work they are made to spin and dress flax. They are commonly very old people. Poor people not absolutely destitute are not taken into the house but receive rations weekly: meal, potatoes and sometimes clothing. They also get knitting and spinning to do and the Poor House gives them money or victuals for their labour. The poor houses are supported by subscribers and annual charity sermons. The Holywood poor house contains about 15 and distributes meal and potatoes weekly to about 30"*.

Before Rev. W.A. Holmes came to Holywood he had been assistant curate of St. Anne's Church in Belfast. In 1808 he wrote a thesis extolling the advantages of Houses of Industry for parishioner and poor. The house he helped to establish in Smithfield had exempted the area *"From the disgrace of overflowing mendicity in eight years"*. In the summer of 1812 he conducted an inquiry in Holywood Parish (Gray point to Connswater River) and discovered 70 destitute families. The following year the Holywood House of Industry was opened on the Marine Parade, on the site of the present-day pedestrian sub-way. Lieutenant Bordes refers to *"Poor House and Cholera Hospital"*. Perhaps the house of industry served as both, however it seems (in 1830) there was a "Cholera House" on Ean Hill or as J.R. Birch always called it *"Ain Hill"*. Cholera reached Europe from Asia in the 1820's. Ireland experienced four major epidemics – 1832, 1848, 1853 and 1866. In the first, that to which Bordes refers, about 25,000 Irish people died, some in the Holywood area.

The House of Industry was forced to terminate its vigilance for the poor when Holywood was incorporated into the Belfast Union. In 1833 Government had established a commission to examine the problem of poverty in Ireland. In 1838 it ignored the findings of the committee and passed the Irish Poor Law. Parishes were grouped into Unions and work houses were built in each Union. Today the campus of Belfast City Hospital covers the grounds of the old Union Work House, into which Holywood had been incorporated. Eventually Holywood House of Industry was demolished. Pleasant little red brick houses with tall yellow chimneys and Gray's Buildings (Q.V.) remained on the vacated site until the 1970's.

According to Surgeon Kelly, Holywood was fortunate in the fact that after 1838, relief continued to be obtained from the Holywood Bequest Fund (founded c. 1771) which at Christmas time distributed blankets and warm clothing to the destitute. The Relief Society provided food and coal during severe winters. Holywood dispensary *"gratuitously afforded advice, medicaments and attendance for the sick and needy"*. The Loan Bank fostered the habits of industry and frugality. Many years later the Holywood Nursing Society added its benevolence to this litany of good works. At the end of the nineteenth century there was a small nursing home or maternity hospital in Hibernia Street. In the 1930's Salernum House on Croft Road was refurbished as a private nursing home with a fine operating theatre. I shall expand the reference to Salernum in a companion volume *"Holywood Houses*

Extant".

Holywood possessed an enlightened and philanthropic conscience long before the advent of State social welfare. The seeds of many of our twenty-first century humanitarian organisations were sown in the eighteenth century.

It is interesting that in Ireland *"Poor House"* was *"House of Industry" "Prisons"* were *"Houses of Correction"*. Recent study in U.S.A. emphasises the optimistic and benign lifestyle of the Scots-Irish immigrants who composed the seven articles of the Constitution (1789), in comparison with general British pessimism. In Ireland the glass is always half full, in England it is half empty!

The House of Industry

XXXI   KILLOP'S COURT (C. 1840) A.P.D.L. 71 HIGH STREET BT18 9AG

In 1917 Lot 36 was Killips Place, the Presbyterian Church and Meneely's Service Garage. On the opposite side of the High Street it included numbers 66 to 72. At that time the tenants were representatives of Rev. Father James O'Laverty (the Church and Numbers 66 to 72 High Street), John McNeely, Alexander Lennox, Charles Patty and Edward Gallagher. The total area was an acre and the annual rent £14.

Robert Read Esq., of the Moat House (see Riverston House Q.V.) acquired numbers 66 to 72 High Street and donated them as a site for the projected St. Colmcille's Parish Church. "Irish Builder" published the architect's drawing of the proposed church alongside the smaller façade of the adjacent Presbyterian Church. When a more eligible site could be obtained for less than the rents arising from his first gift, Mr Read procured the lease of the present ecclesiastical site at the corner of My Lady's Mile and the High Street. Thus the pleasant little terrace (66 to 72 High Street) was saved from destruction in 1872. However, it was demolished in 1999 for the erection of Lesley Mews, an apartment building of ten dwelling units.

Killips Place or Court was a little community all on its own. It was entered through a coach archway between McCourts, the barber's shop and O'Toole's the tailor. Behind McCourt's shop there was a communal rubbish pit which the Council's refuse disposal officers emptied infrequently. A stable belonging to Mr Jimpsy Lennox was set at an angle to the pit; on summer evenings Jimpy gave "The Ladies" pony rides on "Dumpy" around the yard.

Stretching down the hill made by the pre-historic raised beach, was a terrace of five whitewashed houses, each with its black tar skirt – Barrys, Quees, Sullivans, Wiltons and Armstrongs. There were three sheds at the foot of the court – one garaged McNeilly's motor-car, another the Richardsons' motor bike.

The Millers' pretty little cottage, looked straight up Killips Place, with roses round the door which was guarded by two large whitewashed stones. Behind O'Toole's the tailor, Mr Moffat, successor to Dan Barry, operated his blacksmith shop. The high stone wall which bounded Meneely's Motor Service Garage lay beyond the smithy.

In the middle of the cobbled yard a dripping tap supplied the aquatic needs of the little community. It replaced the pump with the cow's tail handle of a previous century.

Such was the picture of Killips Place in the 1930's. Each family has its own fascinating saga well beyond the scope of our present study.

Killip's place or Court was demolished in 1966 to accommodate the extension of Meneely's Service Garage. Today, premises of Consort Travel Group and a car park cover the location.

XXXII TO XXXIV THE KNOCKNAGONEY TRILOGY

CLIFTON, MERTOUN LODGE AND KNOCKNAGONEY HOUSE

1. **Clifton (sometimes called Cliften) (A.P.D.L. Holywood Road, BT18 9QY)**

Clifton House was an eighteenth century mansion built on the raised beach on the east side of Knocknagoney Road The early Ordnance Survey maps indicate a building akin to my pencil sketch. Lieutenant G.F.W. Bordes does not record Clifton under the heading "Modern Topography" (gentlemen's' seats) in his memoirs of 29th September 1834.

Dr. William Haliday was living there in 1783. His son Alexander Henry Haliday was born in Clifton in 1806 and lived there until the 1850's. In 1819 Rev. W.A. Holmes recorded Clifton as *"The seat of Dr. Haliday, three miles and a quarter distant from Belfast South side"*. Alexander Henry Haliday (1806-1870) was Ireland's leading field naturalist. In 1833 he published a thesis based on the insect life of the Holywood area, which he had been observing through all his childhood years at Clifton.

Without a doubt young Henry was familiar with the Holywood Rose (Rosa Hibernica) which grew in profusion on the Knocknagoney shorelands. John Templeton (1766-1828) of Cranmore, the outstanding botanist and author, discovered the hybrid species in 1795 and was given the Dublin Societies' Award. Rev. W.A. Holmes (1819) recorded.

"Templeton's Rose Forms a beautiful bed to near an acre in extent under the road to Richmond Lodge". Road and railway building in the 1840's reduced the plantation to a single hedge. Construction of the Sydenham Roundabout (1970's) decimated the bushes. Fortunately a cutting was taken by Queen's University for the Botanic Gardens. Today the Holywood Rose was returned home and is growing vigorously at "Martello Corner" on Victoria Road.

Surgeon Kelly, writing in 1850, tell us *"Clifton, formerly the residence of the Haliday Family, now is in possession of James Ireland Esq., (Messrs Ireland and McNeill of Corn Market) who enjoys the rewards of honest and persevering industry"*.

The "Honest and Preserving Industry" was the manufacture of cutlery for use on the tables of the high and mighty. Francis Joseph Bigger referred to James Ireland as Belfast's master cutler and made full use of his product. It seems the maker of knives and forks had a family of daughters – "The ten ladies of Clifton". Each young lady had her personal teapot, all of which were brought in by the servants at tea-time and set in a row on the dining room table. Local legend equates the denizens with the parable of the wise and

Head Gardener's Cottage

foolish virgins! By 1858 James Ireland had removed his sorority to "Martello", (where each girl could have her own room as well as tea pot) – while "Oakley" (Q.V.) on Jackson's Road was being built for the family.

After 1858 the Finley family were in residence at Clifton. In 1880 it was demolished and the fine elevated site cleared for the extant Knocknagoney House (Q.V.) According to J.A.K. Dean (1994) Clifton had two gate lodges. The Holywood Lodge, long forgotten, and the Belfast Lodge. The latter served the new Knocknagoney House for many years. Its surrounding area became associated with Orchard Caravans Sales Department. It was torched by vandals and demolished when the lower gardens of Knocknagoney House were used for the erection of a supermarket and car park in 1999.

2. **Mertoun Hall (P.D.L. 106 Belfast Road BT18 9QY)** was a mansion which looked much older than its nineteenth century erection date of 1835 suggests. Fifteen years later Surgeon Kelly recorded *"Mertoun Hall is the residence of John Harrison Esq., J.P., brother of Professor Harrison of Trinity College Dublin, one of the most eminent anatomists of the age. The house is of modern structure, erected some years ago by the present proprietor. It has the disadvantage of being shaded by the extensive and thick plantation which surrounds it"*. The thick plantation contains many special species; at the beginning of the twenty-first century it remains as part of the green belt which must be maintained between Holywood and Belfast.

Tony Merrick (1986) suggests the house was built by a Dr. James Taggart and acquired by the Harrison family about 1838.

John Harrison was agent for the National Assurance Company of Donegall Quay, Belfast. Later he was registered as a ship owner. Before a fortunate removal into the country at Holywood (c.1838), the family boasted a prestigious address at 9 Donegall Square West.

After sixteen years residence at Mertoun, John Harrison acquired the area from the Trustees of John Kennedy

Mertoun Hall

of Holywood House. On 24 October 1854 for £37,000 he bought *"The whole of the rising town of Holywood, private residences, shops, hotels, lands and building ground, including Holywood Demesne, most of Knocknagoney, Priory Park, Kinnegar and Woodlands; Ashfield, Westbrook, Clifton, Maryfield, Richmond, Knockgoney House – in all about 1500 acres producing a gross rental of £1,600."* So in 1854 Mertoun Hall, rather than Holywood House (Q.V.), could have been called the Manor House. Holywood House continued to be the home of another member of the Harrison family. When John Harrison died in 1857. His son Captain John became the squire. He extended and refurbished Mertoun into the style it maintained into the last decades of the twentieth century.

Mertoun Hall had the appearance of a Georgian mansion with extremely wide over hanging eaves and attractive ocult windows in the gables. A broad and pillared open porch guarded the entrance doors which led into a large rectangular main hall. A graceful staircase climbed to the upper floor and on a side table a bowl of apples from the orchard, always tempted young visitors. The reception rooms were extensive and decorated with finest plasterwork. A natural stone pavement bordered the four bay garden façade of the house, it provided a good view over the croquet and tennis lawns. Behind the house there was a huge court-yard completely surrounded by stables, garages, grooms' accommodation and garden rooms. Gates led to a well stocked kitchen garden along the walls of which were extensive stove or greenhouses which produced grapes and peaches for the table in the big house.

There was a pretty little stone built cottage opposite the Holywood Road entrance but a complete absence of the usual pillars and gates. Tony Merrick (1986) suggests that at one time Mertoun Hall shared the grand entrance of Clifton and indeed a footpath thereto is marked on Ordnance Survey maps. This may be explained by the fact that in 1844 Dorothea Kennedy of Holywood House granted John McCance 200 acres of land which did not include the road entrance to his new house. Colonel John McCance had to wait until 1874 to acquire the 51 acres which did include the entrance.

A range of cottages and a large eighteenth century house (extant) completed the extensive Mertoun Hall complex. This house, one of the oldest in the Holywood area, may be the original Knocknagoney House. It is approached by Mertoun back service lane and a disused public footpath from Old Holywood Road.

Hugh McNeile McCormick, donor of Johnny the Jig Playground and former clerk of the Court for County Antrim, claimed that Mertoun Hall (perhaps the earlier house) was the home of the Ross family in 1743, followed by the Kennedys and Dr. Taggart. After the doctor's death about 1840 the house was transferred to John Harrison.

Other Holywood families enjoyed the comfortable life style at Mertoun Hall. Robert Edward McLean, son of James McLean of Plas Merdyn acquired the seven acre park from the Harrison Estate in 1910. R.E. McLean, captain of Trinity College Dublin football club, was capped for Ireland on eleven occasions.

Robert Workman was the next incumbent. He sold the mansion to W.M. May, Esq., Stormont Minister of Education. In January 1958 the auction sale of objects d'art realised £10,000.

Mrs E. McEneaney acquired the property in the 1970's and did not activate planning permission to convert the campus into a private nursing home. The lower part of the park lands were vested to provide a road bridge unto the Belfast Harbour Estate. The house was torched by vandals and completely gutted, although Fire Authority personnel were on site in time to detect the fuel used for the conflagration.

The ruin was acquired by *Esporta*, the most exclusive health club in the Province. The club opened in 2002. Today, fitness arena, dance studios, swimming pool, saunas and spas grace the lawns which gave pleasure in former days to so many Holywood families.

3. **Knocknagoney House (c.1880 108 Belfast Road BT18 9QY)**

Knocknagoney House was erected on the site of Clifton which was demolished in 1880. It was built in the manner of W.H. Lynn. Lynn had been an assistant in the office of the great Charles Lanyon and eventually became a partner in the firm Lanyon, Lynn and Lanyon. Knocknagoney is a massive Victorian essay in red brick, rich in high pointed gables, ostentatious in its position overlooking Belfast Lough.

The mansion's laundry and agricultural buildings were situated in the extant Knocknagoney Farm on Old Holywood Road. Today the buildings are used by Mr Hubert Taylor as a motor service station. The head gardener's house was situated on the Belfast Road and estate workers cottages were built opposite to the entrance gates. Here a cinder path led to Tillysburn Railway Station (B.C.D.R.). Nearby the tracks of the long forgotten Tillysburn light railway harvested seaweed from the mud flats for horticultural purposes.

The McCance family were no strangers to the Knocknagoney area. John McCance, as Trustee for David McCance acquired 200 acres from the Kennedy Estate in 1844. David McCance (and others) received 98 acres from the Harrison Estate in 1866 and John McCance bought a further 51 acres in 1874, also from the Harrison Estate.

John McCance had built a fine house which he called "Suffolk" at Dunmurry in 1824, beside the extensive bleach greens for linen manufacture from which the family accrued its wealth.

Colonel John McCance, J.P., was the best known member of the family. He was a Life Governor of the Royal Victoria Hospital, deeply interested in the early health and safety services of the Castlereagh District Council. The family played a keen part in Holywood social life; children's parties at Knocknagoney were eagerly awaited. Anne McCance, became a proficient Stormont politician and chairperson of the Consumer Council.

In March 1914 Knockmagoney House became one of the North Down residences and Belfast business premises where illicit armaments were cached. The guns were imported from Hamburg to Larne and Donaghadee during the Home Rule revolt. They were hidden for use by the Ulster Volunteer Force when necessary. In July 1914 the National Volunteers landed a smaller supply of guns at Howth. Then in August of that year the Great War broke out, the Home Rule Act was suspended and the Knocknagoney cache remained hidden for many decades.

In 1956 the mansion was refurbished to accommodate the luxurious Windsor Hotel administered by Mr Harry Toner of Holywood. During the 1960's the hotel was a vital element in the growing tourist trade. The troubled times which followed rendered the flourishing business inoperable.

The Northern Ireland Police Authority acquired the property in 1978 and continue to use it for educational purposes into the twenty first century. In 1999 the lower part of the extensive pleasure gardens became the site of an extensive supermarket with car parks and service station.

XXXV LORNE (1873) P.D.L. STATION ROAD BT18 OBP

GUIDE ASSOCIATION HEADQUARTERS

As a young lad Henry James Campbell (1813-1889) was apprenticed to Messrs James Dorman and Company, Flax Spinners of Belfast. He became partner and director of the Mossley Mills – linen thread manufacturers and Messrs. Gunning and Campbell, flax spinners of North Howard Street.

This merchant prince resigned from an exceptionally active business life in 1873 to reside with his sisters at Lorne House, which he had built for his retirement years. The lease had been obtained from Sir Robert Kennedy on 30 June 1873, building commenced immediately. The house was named after the traditional home of the Clan Campbell in Scotland. The ancestral emblem, a wild boar's head, is emblazoned at Lorne and the college which Henry James Campbell founded at Belmont. Campbell College was endowed with a £200,000 bequest.

H.J. Campbell desired that a school or a hospital be built in his name *"or to abandon either to benefit the other"*. Before 1890, Belmont House and the seventy acre parkland were acquired from Sir Thomas McClure for the College campus, the quadrangle of which indicates the site of Belmont House.

H.J. Campbell, a life long bachelor died in his grand seaside house on 23 January 1889, aged 76. His two unmarried sisters continued to reside at Lorne for the remainder of their lives.

The house lay vacant for some time, then towards the end of the war years the Board of Governors of Campbell College decided to sell Lorne. The school was coming home from evacuation to Portrush; it was a time of financial restrictions and funding was required for a building project at Cabin Hill.

At that time the Guide Association was searching for a suitable location in which to establish a training camp. On 14 October 1944 the committee "found" Lorne; the following month a decision to purchase the estate was taken. The Trustees agreed to sell the house with its 21 acres of park lands for £6,000.

Holywood Town Hall (1876), Sullivan National School (1862), Sullivan Upper School (1877) and Lorne House (1873) were built in the fashionable material of the period – yellow polychrome brickwork relieved by dark yellow sandstone.

The garden front of Lorne has five extended bays, two large bay windows divided by a projecting curvilinear gable which carries a turreted circular bay window on the first storey. The quoined mansion has a four-storey circular tower surmounted by a balustrade. The long pillared porch on the entrance front is crenellated and carries a balustrade with spherical finials. The Victorian windows carry drip-courses; the tall chimneys are doubled or tripled on plinths.

On the west façade the magnificent wrought iron conservatory, which the Campbell family greatly enjoyed, has been carefully restored and compares favourably with the Palm House in Botanic Gardens.

The central entrance hall, the grand staircase with its fine casements, and the stucco work in the main reception rooms are exceptionally good.

Near the entrance gates, H.J. Campbell built a triple cottage block, in the same style as mansion house. Today these, like the house itself, are in pristine condition, thanks to the Province of Ulster Guides Association.

XXXVI TO XXXIX FOURSOME OF MANSES GLENSIDE, BEECH-CROFT GLENAVON AND CHURCHILL

1. **First Holywood Presbyterian Church (1615) P.D.L. Glenside Manse (c.1850) 79 Victoria Road, BT18 9BG.**

During the ministry of Rev. John King (1754-1777), the manse was situated in the old Market Square opposite the hotel. In 1850 Surgeon Kelly advised his promenanders and rusticators *"To direct their steps on some fine summer day to the Ballykeel Road and the Holywood Hills. Soon the Glen yields a variety of subjects, which may not be exhausted in one nor in many hours of attentive observation. A few perches brings us opposite the beautiful little cottage, "Glenside" the residence of Rev. Henry Henderson"*.

Rev. Henry Henderson was inducted into the charge in 1844 and died in 1879. In August 1855 the Kirk session decided to acquire a congregational manse. However, it was not until 1878 that Henry Henderson was paid £600 for his *"beautiful little cottage"*. Perhaps at that time it was extended into a commodious residence. The frontal annex provides additional bedrooms, a spacious drawing room, a study, entrance and staircase halls. The older part of the house retains a family room and extensive kitchen, offices – one of which is a "secret room". The stable block was situated between the Manse and the Ballykeel River. The river could be diverted through the spacious grounds to conduct water to the mill dam at Martello Corner. The conduit is extant and the culverted channel runs beneath the Victoria Road footpath.

Glenside Manse served the congregation for about 150 years. In 1996 it was sold and part of the orchard used to build a new house. Today historic old Glenside is meticulously maintained by Simon Bridge and Irene Kingston as a private residence.

2. **First Holywood Presbyterian Church (Non-Subscribing) (1615) – Beechcroft Manse (1864) P.D.L. 18 Croft Road, BT18 OPB**

It cannot be said with any certainty where the Holywood clergy resided after the Reformation. Perhaps the Priory House was available for the Dissenting Ministers who served the parish until 1661.

The Rev. C.J. McAlester was inducted into the non-subscribing charge in 1834. In 1864 he built a comfortable Victorian manse in an extended acre park on the sunnyside of the recently made Croft Road. It was purchased by the congregation after his death for the following incumbent Rev. C.E. Pike. The fine house continued to be Beechcroft Manse until the retirement of Rev. C.M. Kelly, then it was demolished and the site used for the four exclusive neo-Georgian residences called Croft Meadows.

The Old Manse was a square house with several spacious reception rooms all furnished with fine marble fireplace surrounds. One of the rooms had elegant full length french windows opening unto the west lawns. A canted bay window with pilasters and cornice overlooked the lawns. The hipped roof carried three broad chimney stacks. A wide string course surrounded the building. The doorcase was exceptionally fine, again with pilasters and cornice. All sash windows had four vertical panes – an unusual feature for a house of its age.

3. High Street Presbyterian Church (1858). Glenavon Manse P.D.L. 25 Church Avenue BT18 9BJ

The First Minister, Rev, J.S. Denham, was installed in the new Church on the High Street in 1858. In 1873 Glenavon, a private residence on Church Avenue, was purchased by the congregation as the manse from Mrs Anna D. Milliken. The grand black basalt stone building completed the line of mansions which overlooked the Ballykeel River. Twistle Bridge (1912) and its approaches, a memorial to Richard Patterson, (former Chairman of the Urban Council) wended its way around the eastern perimeter of the manse grounds.

During the long Ministry of Rev. Dr. Maconaghie an interesting rock and scree garden was laid out between the house and the river. In the summer terms all staff and pupils of Sullivan Upper School were given a special garden party in the manse grounds.

In 1997 'Glenavon' was sold and a house acquired in Norwood Lane for the resident clergy.

4. The Methodist Church (1838) Churchill Manse, 10/12 Church View BT18 9DP

The Church Trustees report for January 1886 records *"Holywood is now in course of acquiring a manse – a very eligible and desirable house standing in its own grounds".*

It seems this was the house already rented for Rev. Hugh McGabie. In December a deed was registered between *"Eileen Cooper of Holywood House and Dublin and the Trustees, on behalf of the Society of people called Methodists for the sale of Church Hill, with the green house and garden, for £625 freehold".* Mrs Cooper had lived in one of the semi-detached villas. When she removed to Dublin she rented her property to the Methodist Church. Archibald Sloan lived in the other house.

The lovely old house at Churchill served the congregation well. In June 1953 it was sold for £800. Rev R.F.C. Rooney removed to 22 My Lady's Mile in December 1952. "Somerset" continues to be the Methodist Manse into the new millennium. Churchill was demolished in the year 2000.

XL MARINE COTTAGE (ORIGINALLY BUILT IN EIGHTEENTH CENTURY)
MARINE PARADE P.D.L. THROUGHPASS BT18 9HY

A photograph taken by W. Lawrence (1878) shows the long thatched single-storey cottage, set in a garden shaded by ancient trees and surrounded by white-washed walls. The early maps mark buildings on the site. The 1883 map of the Harrison Estate shows an extensive building with sizeable back premises on a half –acre garden with two greenhouses. In 1917 Hugh McCormick was the tenant; a lease dated 11 December 1843 was granted by John Harrison to C.K. Cordner and James Sefton (Rent £20.00).

Possibly the original buildings were the cottages of local sailors and fisherfolk. Opposite the front gate a jetty stretched into the lough. At that time Marine Parade bordered the golden sands of Holywood's fine bathing beaches. The railway line to Bangor did not intrude until 1865.

After the cottages became a single unit, the well-known Emerson family were in residence. Surgeon Kelly (1850) refers to *"Marine Cottage" on Marine Parade as a favourable resort of parties requiring a summer residence"*.

One of *"The parties"* was the Batt Family of Purdysburn House. Narcissus Batt was the founder of the Belfast Bank (1827). It seems the family favoured our fashionable seaside town for summer holidays, before the railway line bisected Marine Parade. The Batts were related to the Turnlys of Richmond Lodge (Q.V.) and Rockport House (Q.V.). No doubt family bathing parties were organised from this seaside cottage.

Possibly Marine Cottage was one of the earliest groups of buildings in Holywood. It was demolished in 1970 to make way for the Holywood Throughpass. In 1956 Holywood Urban District Council hoped to save our heritage by utilising a sea-board route for the Bangor Dual Carriageway to by-pass the town. The Department for the Environment thought otherwise!

The venue of Marine Cottage was used as part of Hibernia Street Car Park for three decades. It became a building site at the beginning of the twenty-first century.

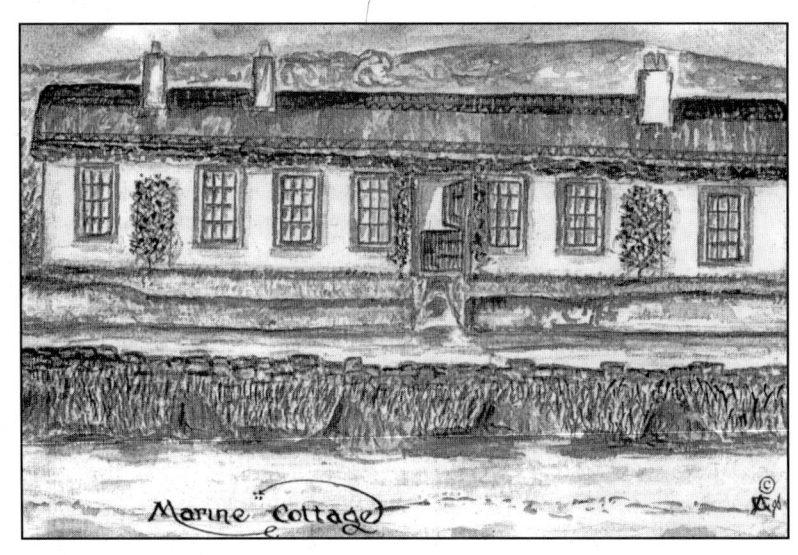

XLI THE MARINE HOTEL (C. 1840'S) MARINE PARADE BT18 9HY

A.P.D.L. THROUGHPASS

Surgeon Kelly (1850) records an advertisement for Holywood as the top sea-side summer retreat. *"Ample accommodation, in the first style is provided at the Marine Hotel, for those whose brief sojourn disincline them to encumber themselves by the cares of house keeping or with a separate establishment. At the Marine Hotel unfailing attention and civility have attracted a large concourse of the highest respectability of strangers and visitors. At the hotel there has been established an American Bowling Alley, which simple amusement is abundantly practised; we are informed that the village now contains many players of no mean proficiency"*.

The health giving sea-bathing which Kelly advocates was a few steps from the hotel's front door, along the sandy beaches on the southern shores of Belfast Lough. Perhaps "The Marine" closed down because the railway destroyed its beach-side position. A photograph (taken by W. Lawrence), shows the building had been converted to semi-detached residences by 1878.

The property appears under Lot 62 in the sale of head rents (1917). At that time the tenant was James Lennox. A lease dated 14 June 1871 was granted by John Harrison to William Bottomly, for almost one acre of seaside land at £30.00. per annum. Probably William Bottomly built the hotel in the 1840's. The Seven Bay symmetrical façade contained a central gate way with arch through which carriages were admitted to the extensive rear suite of buildings, which extended to a small sheltered garden. No doubt one of offices accommodated "the American Bowling Alley". When the building was converted into domestic dwellings two entrances were created in the perimetrical bays.

The lot included the villa which adjoined the hotel. It seems this was the house to which Bernard Hughes Esq. (1808-1878) brought his family in the 1840's. Bernard Hughes was founder and owner of Ireland's premier bakery. The family removed to College Square in 1855. He retired to Riverston House (Q.V.) on Church Road in 1872.

By 1860 John Getty McGee Esq., was living in the villa. He was proprietor of Belfast's leading merchant tailors in High Street. His skill at outfitting put the Province on the world map of fashion with the famous 'Ulster' coat, to which he gave that name in 1867. Soon it *"gained universal patronage in America, India, amid the snows of Russia, in Turkey and in England where a warm and waterproof wrapper is desideratum"*.

In 1855 J.G. McGee organised the Holywood Warf Scheme to provide a new jetty for the sea front. The major subscribers were Captain John Harrison £50.00, Henry Harrison £30.00 and the Holywood railway company £20.00.

The 150 feet wooden jetty cost £257.19. The use of the facility cost half-a crown, except for local fishermen who gave a couple of days each year to desilt the channel.

On 8 May 1867 J. G. McGee called for three cheers, when the good ship Erin made her inaugural call at the big brother of the little wharf – the 1000 feet Holywood Pier. Happy days in historic Holywood, where every old house has a story to recite!

XLII MARMION LODGE C. 1858

P.D.L. MARMION ADOLESCENT UNIT 136 CHURCH ROAD BT18 9BZ

In the sale of Holywood town ground rents (1917) Lot 70 recorded a lease dated 29 January 1858 to John Burgoyne (rental £26.00). Stanley House (Q.V.), Marmion Lodge and Chester (now Rialto) were built on the site.

Lot 71, 4 acres lying between Church Road and the Ballykeel River, was held by John Burgoyne. It included the path from Church Avenue to the Twistle Bridge. The east side of the path became the lower part of Marmion's grounds, the west side became an addition to the gardens of Rialto, where the Garratt family lived.

The remaining lots on Church Avenue are of interest. Lot 74, Craigmore (one acre) was leased to James Williamson, the tenant was Robert Garratt Esq. Lot 75 was Glenavon Manse (Q.V.), lease dated 5 Seprember 1867 to Anna D. Milliken. Conveniently, the second part of Lot 75 (26 December 1857) was the campus of High Street Presbyterian Church.

John Burgoyne built Marmion Lodge in 1858. It seems the first family to live there were the Greens. Foster Green owned the well-known United Kingdom Tea Blending Company. A hospital on Saintfield Road, Belfast originally for patients recovering from pulmonary tuberculosis, memorializes the famous Foster Green name.

In more recent years the Boyd Family and then the Parsons enjoyed the spacious old house. Both families contributed greatly to the special Holywood ambience and the prosperity of the Province.

Originally a square building, at some time an extra wing was added to the rear of the east façade. Externally the impressive decoration included quoins, balustrades, string courses and heavy label mouldings over both square and circular headed windows. Internally the several reception rooms were highly ornamented.

Marmion's grounds extended to 4 acres beyond the elaborate entrance gates; one of the notable features of which was the kitchen garden. Parts of its old brick walls continue to shield numbers 1-19 Church Avenue, which were built on the site.

In 1953, Marmion became a children's home. The beautiful mansion was demolished in 1979. At that time the children were removed into the adjoining property, Stanley House (Q.V.), while the present Marmion Adolescent Unit was under construction. In turn, its demolition is proposed for 2003 – to make way for a purpose built unit.

The lower parts of the grounds have been used for New Croft House and Twisel Lodge. New Croft House is a purpose built home for the elderly confused. In Twisel Lodge the Karen Mortlock Trust organises a home for young people with severe disabilities. Twisel Lodge was officially opened in May 1994.

Before we turn to the story of Maryfield, I shall add a few words on the river and bridge which are situated close to Marmion.

The pseudonymous *"Twisel River"* took this spurious name from Twisel Bridge, a structure over the River Till, a tributary of the River Tweed, the boundary between Scotland and England. Here the battle of Flodden was fought on 9 September 1513. The English Army commanded by the Earl of Surrey defeated the Scots, who were led by King James himself. The King and ten thousand of his followers were cut down on Flodden Moor. The Earl of Surrey won the battle by keeping Sir Edward Stanley and the Palatine of Chester on his left wing.

In Holywood, the Ballykeel River ran under the Kissing Bridge. When the literary works of Sir Walter Scott (1771 – 1832) became popular, an old Holywood tradition came to mind – The Ballykeel River divided the Scottish and English settlements in the seventeenth century.

In his poem "Marmion" Scott records:

*"From Flodden Ridge
The Scots beheld the English Host
Leave Barmore-wood, their evening post
And heedful watched them as they cross'd
The Till by Twisel Bridge.
High sight it is, and haughty while
They dive into the deep defile" (XIX of Canto VI)*

Towards the end of the battle, when the defiant Lord Marmion lies dying, Scott writes:

*"The war, that for a space did fail,
Now trebly thundering swell'd the gale,
And – Stanley! was the cry;
A light on Marmion's visage spread,
And fired his glazing eye:
With dying hand, above his head,
He shook the fragment of the blade,
And shouted "Victory"
Charge, Chester, Charge! On, Stanley On!
Were the last words of Marmion (XXXII of Canto VI)*

In Holywood the three houses which were built on the banks of the Ballykeel River took the names Chester, Stanley (Q.V.) and Marmion (Q.V.).

In the notes to 'Marmion' (1808) Scott recorded *"The ancient Bridge of Twisel, by which the English crossed the Till is still standing beneath Twisel Castle. The Glen is romantic and delightful, with steep banks on each side covered with copse, particularly with hawthorn. Beneath a tall rock near the bridge, is a plentiful fountain".*

All of which is reminiscent of the Glenlyon ravine through which the Ballykeel River flows, before it is crossed by the Kissing Bridge.

Marmion Lodge

XLIII MARYFIELD (C.1830) P.D.L. 104 BELFAST ROAD BT19 9QY

NORTHERN IRELAND OFFICE

Maryfield was built in the 1830's, the first resident was John Kennedy Esq. In 1840 John Heron Esq. (1781-1870) bought the property, the Heron family remained in residence for the next 130 years.

John Heron was one of the founders of the Ulster Bank (1836); with that financial institution the family maintained its links for over a century.

An original Grant in Fee dated 22 July 1674 described the 50 acre demesne; another dated 6 May 1840 noted Dorothia Kennedy's grant to John Heron. In 1917, the representatives of John Heron remained tenants under the title Lot 1, total rent £10.00 per annum. It is interesting to discover that the first lot contained land at Redburn, Ardtullagh and *"Path etc. at Sea Wall"*. In fact the Maryfield Demesne extended to the lough shores.

Surgeon Kelly (1850) described the house: *"Maryfield is the commodious and picturesque residence of John Heron Esq., one of Belfast's princely merchants. The grounds, although not extensive, are well disposed, and an extensive view of Belfast Lough and the opposite shore of Antrim, with its hill and dale and woodland scenery, is here obtained"*.

The house was built in the neo-classical style. The hipped roof was completely surrounded by a high balustrade interspersed by piers carrying large ball finials with spires. Similar ornaments appeared on the large porch with its semi-circular headed windows and door case. The five bays carried string courses and quoins.

The west or garden façade sported a large bay window on the ground floor, which illuminated the second sitting room. The interior was approached through a wide central hallway which led to a broad staircase, the extensive return landing of which was top lighted and displayed fine examples of Roasmund Praeger's work. This art collection had been assembled by Miss Mary Heron, local philanthropist, who was the last member of the family to live at Maryfield.

Various service offices extended beyond the capacious kitchens into a yard. Some 50 metres to the south of the main house yard was a court yard accommodating equestrian and agricultural buildings. To the west was a large kitchen garden with a high red brick wall and a pretty little dovecote at the entrance gate.

The gate lodge was octagonal, its alternate faces projected semi-circular headed windows and a similar doorcase with fanlight. The octahedral roof was crowned with a octagonal chimney stack, carrying a tall pot. The lodge and convex quadrant entrance-gate walls were demolished for road works in the 1970's. On the opposite side of the Holywood to Belfast Road there was a plain two storey cottage, in the early years of the twentieth century it was occupied by the head gardener of Knocknagoney House.

Maryfield was torched by vandals in 1969. The park was acquired for commercial purposes and later for use by the Northern Ireland Office, when direct rule form the Palace of Westminister was restored to the Province on 25 March 1972.

XLIV NUMBER TWENTY EIGHT, THE HIGH STREET (C. 1870) A.P.D.L. HEALTH CENTRE AND PRIORY SURGERY BT18 9AD

Originally Number 28 was a pair of semi-detached residences without a name, which was very unusual in Holywood. It was set well back behind the building line of High Street and overlooked the Old Market Square.

There was a long front garden and even longer gardens extending to the Ballykeel River with the Crescent on its south bank. The back garden was a forest of magnificent hydrangeae, white, pink and blue. The front gardens were beautifully maintained as a joy to passers-by on the High Street.

At some time the semi-detached houses were redesigned into a single dwelling. The party wall on the ground floor was broken into arches to provide a double hallway. One of the door case openings was converted to a window, providing additional illumination to the rather unusual square hall.

The drawing room was on the left, the dining room on the opposite side. Behind the reception rooms were parallel suites of sitting rooms, kitchens, sculleries and garden rooms. The two staircases remained intact and climbed beside each other to the first floor where party walls were removed to make long dark corridors. The master bedroom and the nursery with dressing rooms were to the front of the house. Behind these was a collection of bathrooms and bedrooms.

Steep stairs led to the attics, were children were not allowed to venture. *"Up there were storerooms and domestic quarters"*. Number 28 was a plain stuccoed six bay building with quoins, tall chimney stacks and twelve pane Georgian windows.

This was the home of the Pattersons, and well remembered by little Betty who married Jim Shannon – a union of two of the best known Holywood families.

In the 1950's the Holywood Urban District Council acquired the house for community purposes. The front garden was used to accommodate public toilets. After demolition in the 1970's the site was used for Holywood Health Centre. Eventually Priory Surgery was added to the complex.

In the 1917 sale, the lease for number 28 was Lot 78 dated 1871, John Harrison to David Lennox. Strangely, the second part of Lot 78 was the houses opposite the old fountain in Church Road, beside the gate to the Methodist Church.

XLV OAKLEY (1858) A.P.D.L. 50 BELFAST ROAD, BT18 9EL. OFFICERS QUARTERS
PALACE MILITARY BARRACKS

On 17 April 1858 James Ireland, a previous resident of Clifton (Q.V.) was granted nine acres of the Holywood Demesne by Henry Harrison. The area was bounded by the Belfast and Jackson Roads.

The 1819 Belfast Directory described James Ireland as Ironmonger and Tin Plate Manufacturer of Cornmarket, Belfast. By the 1850's he was a shipowner and the city's leading Master Cutler.

James Ireland died in the mid 1870's and was interred in the old Cliften Street Graveyard. The Misses Ireland continued to live at Oakley.

By 1906, Letitia and Sarah appear to be the tenants of Oakley, paying an annual rent of £84.00. Letitia died on 2 September 1906. The following month Sarah Ireland and John Milliken, Trustees of James Ireland's will, bought Oakley from the land commission for £2050 (Folio 4267, to be repaid at £16.12.6 half yearly).

On 5 September 1916, Louisa Ireland, then a widow, became the owner of Oakley. The property did not feature in the sale of Holywood head rents on 4 December 1917.

Four years later, 14 September 1920, William Boyd, the Managing Director of Harland and Wolff Ltd., brought his family to live at Oakley. Molly, Dorothy, Eileen and Sheila. So another family of young ladies raised the old roof with their laughter! William Boyd died on 11 January 1934.

Ten months later (12 November 1934) James E Anderson, director of Anderson and McAuley Ltd, bought Oakley for £1,650. Messrs Anderson and McAuley Ltd was an extensive city centre department store. In the 1960's the directors expanded the business to "Supermac" on the outer ring road. It became A.J. Sainsbury's Shopping Centre. James Anderson died on 19th September 1941 leaving the property to his widow, Ivy Marguerite. However, by that time the War Department had requisitioned Oakley House (6 May 1940 rental £160). Five months later (19 October 1940) the Oakley lands were requisitioned (rental £20.00 per annum). During the war years the house was used as an officers mess for the regiments stationed at Palace Barracks.

On 23 September 1949, the Secretary of State for War purchased Oakley for £6150. The annuity was redeemed for £1275 on 3 August 1950. The Holywood Urban District Council and the Ministry of Commerce acquired one half acre of the lands for commercial purposes.

Married officers quarters were built on the Oakley lands between 1953 and 1975. In 1974 a wooden annex to the Officers Mess was erected to accommodate the increased strength required by the 1969 emergency in the Province.

In June 1978 Oakley House was declared to be in a dangerous condition by the Property Service Agency. It was demolished three months later (September 1978).

Oakley was a great square mansion in the neo-classical style. The corniced eaves carried a consoled and panelled frieze. Pilaster quoins on the ground floor led to moulded quoins on the second floor. A small cannon defended the central ground floor bay, which was surmounted by a pair of semi-circular windows. These were paralleled by the windows of the west facing porch.

The three great reception rooms which overlooked the lough were decorated with very fine plaster work, marble fireplaces and extensive carpentry. A decorative staircast with cash iron balustrade rose from the large central hall below a hemispherical dome.

In front of the house there was a carefully tended tennis and croquet lawn and to the south a court yard was surrounded on three sides with stables and gardens. A walled kitchen garden lay beyond the courtyard. During the war years the gardens were tended by inmates from the nearby prisoner of war camp.

Further description of Oakley is recorded in the companion volume 'Holywood Then and Now'. The essay 'A Garrison Town' includes reference to the Bishop's Palace (Q.V.) Westbrook and Oakley, the pleasure grounds of which houses are the present day campus of the Palace Military Barracks.

Oakley House

XLVI O'NEILL'S PLACE (C. 1840) A.P.D.L. 21 CHURCH ROAD BT18 9BU

O'NEILL'S PLACE APARTMENT BUILDING

Lot 95 in the 1917 sale recorded the representatives of William Neeson as the tenants of O'Neill's Place. The lease is dated 20 September 1892 – C.R. Cordner (First Part) John Harrison (Second Part) and William Neeson (Third Part); it granted a mere twenty-one perches for the comparatively high annual ground rent of £22.

Of course, the Place goes back much further than 1892, probably to the 1840's. Entrance was obtained by an arch between numbers 21 and 23 Church Road, two pretty little two-storey houses, the back premises of which opened into O'Neill's Place.

It seems there were four cottages in O'Neill's place, however in the memory of those who lived there in the early twentieth century, there were two houses on the south side of the little court yard and stables, barns and storage offices to the north. Possibly these started life as small dwellings. One of the early residents was William Neeson, local builder and carpenter. He crafted the ecclesiastical furnishings for the old Church of St. Colmcille. William's daughter Mary, who was born in O'Neill's Place, painted the Celtic lettering of the Altus Prosator which surrounded the beautiful building.

Along the west boundary, a high stone wall divided O'Neill's Place from the gardens of Sweeney's Medical Hall on the High Street. The Sweeney family lived in the large house beside the pharmacy, the garden of which was meticulously tended. A pear tree was trained along the wall which divided the garden from O'Neill's place. One day a stone near the foot of the wall was seen to move, a hand appeared, a large and juicy pear disappeared and the stone immediately returned into place.

The next time the hand materialised the young master of the Sweeney household was waiting to make sure it would never reappear. His strategem was successful!

The pleasant little court yard, the Church Road houses on either side of the arched gateway and the fine 1894 building on its north side, (Ted's fruit and vegetable Emporium) were demolished in the 1980's to make way for the present day O'Neill's Place – which is an apartment building providing 24 dwelling units.

During the nineteenth century Holywood rejoiced in ten little enclaves, now only three remain. Here is a list of Holywood's Courts and Entries.

1. O'Neill's Place
2. Patton's Lane (Q.V.)
3. Killop's (Killips) Place (Q.V.)
4. Stewarts Court (31-33 Shore Road) Seven houses built about 1860)
5. Alexandra Place (High Street) Extant (Originally four houses)
6. Gray's Court (High Street) nine houses, L-shaped; demolished in 1921 to make way for the present day First Trust Bank.
7. Gray's Lane (High Street Number 111) built about 1830 – partly extant – set at an angle.
8. Wilson's Lane (Church Road) nine houses, set at an angle, removed c.1860 to accommodate Sullivan Street which was demolished in 1969 for car parking.
9. Byron Place (Kinnegar) extant.
10. The Bandroom Vennel (between 83 or 85 High Street).

XLVII PATTON'S LANE P.D.L. BETWEEN HUGH STREET AND CHURCH VIEW

BT18 9HN AND 9DB

The pedestrian entrance to Patton's Lane is situated between numbers 82 and 84, High Street. Formerly the Old Palace Bar, Ernest Allan's Chemists shop and Tog's Ice Cream Parlour surrounded the arched approach. Back in the 1850's Surgeon Thomas T. Kelly had his premises nearby; he gave us our first history book on Holywood, from which frequently I have quoted in these volumes.

The pretty little gravelled close was home to a happy community of Holywood families.

On the west side two pebble dashed houses belonged to the Cardys and the Boyles. Then came a gateway which was marked by a large stone. This gate took the speculator into the local turf accountant's office. The Moores, the Pollards and the Hughes lives in the adjoining terrace.

Beside the Church View entrance, two houses looked down the lane, set at a right angle to the neighbouring dwellings. Here the Churchman and McCullough families resided. The first of these buildings became a hall where the local band held practises; for many years the other was a very interesting antique shop. Now both houses are in a ruinous condition.

To the west side of Patton's Lane, Jonathan Jefferson's "Old Palace Bar" extended from the High Street, its wide back gates opened into the lane. The first floor of the Palace Bar provided a large assembly hall where the Order of Buffalos held meetings.

The houses on the east side of the lane were replaced with a line of shops: a turf accountants, taxi office and various passing entrepreneurs. On the opposite side a shoe shop operated for many years.

In the 1917 sale of the town, Patton's Lane came under Lot 40. The tenant was Jonathan Jefferson. The original lease for thirty perches of land was granted by Dorothea Kennedy to David Patton, dated 5 May 1834 at £8 per annum.

The Patton's Lane property has potential to become an exclusive enclave of specialist shops. Its refurbishment would enhance the ambience of the town centre.

In 2002 such a scheme was prepared by Q.U.B.

XLVIII PEBBLE LODGE (c.1870) P.D.L. THE PARKS APARTMENT BUILDING
BELFAST ROAD (BT18 9ES)

Lot 109 was the most inscrutable item in the sale of Holywood Head-Rents offered in Messrs R.J. McConnell's Royal Avenue auction rooms on 4 December 1917. It listed 16 areas amounting to 12 acres (total rents £244.10) scattered all over the town.

The sites included small items in Hibernia Street, Church View, Church Road, High Street; a long strip which ran through the present campus of Priory College; a sizeable rectangle situated in the middle of the golf links; another narrow strip which ran along the back gardens between St. Colmcilles Church and The Firs.

The most important division of Lot 109 was a three acre section lying between the former cricket grounds and Bellevue Terrace. The lease was dated 12 June 1871, John Harrison to Samuel Patton for 999 years, rental £23.9s. At that time tenancy was held by James and Hugh Patton, whose names appeared on all the divisions of Lot 109. Today the major portion is covered by the Rugby Club, the North Down Borough Council's allotments of garden plots and the grounds of Bellevue Terrace which was erected in the 1840's. Pebble Lodge appeared to have been built shortly after the Patton family acquired Lot 109, section 4 in 1871.

It was a charming cottage residence approached by broad steps on the west entrance front. To the east the cottage became a two-storey building. The high ceilinged drawing room was the most impressive room in the house. The four windowed bays came to floor level and originally commanded a panoramic view over Ireland's first golf course to the lough and the blue hills of Antrim. The scope of view was enhanced as the cottage was built on the prehistoric raised beach.

Pebble Lodge was unlike any other house in Holywood and appeared much younger than its 1870 date, perhaps it is best described as Victorian Gothic revival in style. It was more akin to a Mediterranean or Killiney sea-side lodge and should have been preserved as a North Down treasure. Before demolition (1997) it was in excellent condition.

The house had triple diagonally set chimney stacks, quoins, stepped label moulded drip courses, gable triangular arched windows, three multi-windowed bays, elaborate purlin ends, decorative fascia and x-ed cartouche beneath the east facing windows. The whole property was dashed with large pebbles.

There was a large yard and service area pointing towards the entrance gates and extensive grounds before the front garden.

The Taylors were the best known Holywood family to live in Pebble Lodge. Samuel C. Taylor was a talented designer and professional Ulster artist; his daughter Anne was a competent water colourist. Both worked from a purpose-built north lighted studio building which adjoined the Lodge. The studio intrigued junior pupils of Sullivan Upper School, the campus of which is on the opposite side of Belfast Road.

Pebble Lodge was a rare example of Irish Victorian architecture. It was demolished in November 1997. The Parks, an apartment building containing eighteen units, was erected on the vacated site.

Pebble Lodge

XLIX REDBURN (1866) A.P.D.L. OLD HOLYWOOD ROAD BT18 9QH

HOLYWOOD NURSING HOME

Robert Grimshaw Dunville (1838-1910) chose well the site for a new mansion, when he left the family home, Richmond Lodge (Q.V.) to enjoy married life with the charming Jeanie Chaine (1842-1914).

The new house was built in Fiddler's Field on the old Holywood Road; an older dwelling had to be removed before the mansion could be erected on the 170 acres site. R.G. Dunville may have helped to draw the elaborate plans; as a youth he may have spent some time on the staff of Sir Charles Lanyon – Ulster's premier architect. That R.G. was a gifted artist is shown by sketches which illustrate two of his private publications: *"North Sea Bubbles"* and *"The Norseman Pilot's Song"*. The poems describe cruises on *"The Black Pearl"* – a steam yacht of 343 tons *"with 25 hands on board"*, sailing out of Cultra.

Lanyon, Lynn and Lanyon designed the seventy rooms mansion, the erection of which cost over £28,000 in 1866. Constructed of finest Scrabo stone, it commanded panoramic views over Belfast Lough and was set against the splendid scenery of the Holywood Hills. The most spectacular rooms were the ballroom with Waterford crystal chandelier and the rectangular entrance hall with memorial window to John Spenser Dunville, V.C. (1896-1917). Bedrooms were en-suite, a century before that term became customary. I remember visiting the unoccupied house shortly after the estate was acquired by the Holywood Urban District Council in 1950 for £14,700 Some of the rooms in the comfortable staff wing had never been used – woodwork and plaster walls were undecorated – exactly as the builders had left them in 1866!

Heated glass houses produced out of season exotic fruits for the table, a vast conservatory provided flowers for all seasons. A separate laundry building served the needs of family and guests, a neat little dairy produced butter and cream from the herd of Jersey cows. In the park there were bridle paths, tennis courts, a palm shaded water garden, several ornamental cascades, special horticultural collections and a purpose built kennel house for the pack of hounds, beagles and German shepherd dogs.

In 1879 a separate walled court yard and stable yard with elegant clock tower was added to the campus. Apartments were provided for the team of fourteen grooms. The court was build of red sandstone specially imported from Scotland. With the main gate lodge, the courtyard remains extant. The lodge, consistent with the house, enhanced the grand entrance gates at the junction of Demesne Road and Jackson's Road. A traditional Irish cottage lodge dominated the Belfast gates with a couple of thatched houses on the west side of the sphere finialied pillars. About 1920 a private zoo was laid out behind the house – its walls remain into the twenty-first century.

Colonel John Dunville, C.B.E. (1866-1929) inherited Redburn and the Royal Irish Distillery. It was a great day for the house when John brought his bride home from Beau Park, County Meath. Violet Anne Blanche Lambert was a granddaughter of the Marquis Conyngham. The new Mrs Dunville introduced a life-style to Redburn which led the Province in opulence, until the Royal Irish Distillery went into voluntary liquidation in the depression years of the mid 1930's.

After Violet's death in 1940 the house was commandeered by the Air Ministry. After the war the Holywood Urban District acquired the entire estate. Holywood people fantasized a cottage hospital and a youth centre with theme parks! In reality parts of the lands were used for cemetery, sporting and educational purposes. The mansion house was vandalised and demolished; the site was acquired by the Bradford Family for the construction of a hotel. It turned out to be an unsuccessful business venture and British Petroleum bought the ugly bunker like building in order to establish a staff members' club. In turn the club building was demolished and Holywood Private Nursing Home built where Redburn House had dominated the Holywood Hills for over a century. When local government was reorganised in 1973; the remaining 120 acres of Parklands had to be transferred to the Department for the Environment. Today it is the prestigious Redburn Country Park which attracts thousands of visitors every year.

The story of the Dunville Family is recorded in the companions volume "Holywood Then and Now" in the essay entitled "Whiskey Galore".

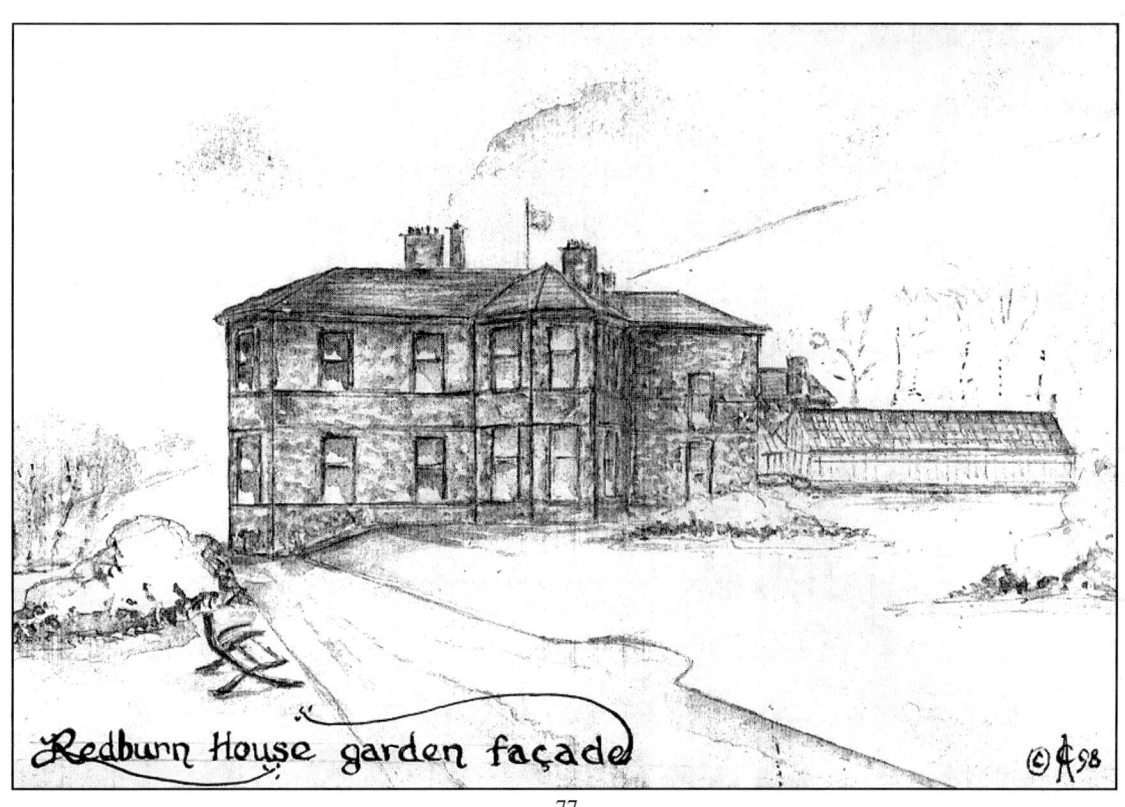

Holywood Gate Lodge

Redburn House garden façade

Redburn House

Front Porch

Belfast Gate Cottages

L REDBURN SQUARE NUMBER SEVEN BT18 9HZ

7 Redburn Square (formerly Hibernia Street) was part of Lot 29 in the 1917 sale of the town. John Harrison granted a lease dated 19 February 1874 to Austin Waters for nine and a quarter perches at six guineas per annum. To this was added four perches by memorandum.

Another part of Lot 29 was reserved to the owner for an ornamental plot. Eventually the garden became Redburn Square, after the erection of the Holywood War Memorial in 1922.

Austin Waters, who was head constable of the Royal Irish Constabulary, built his tall town house in 1875. In later years he became Clerk to the Holywood Town Commissioners. When Austin Waters died in 1904 he gave the house to his dutiful daughter Harriet, with bequests to four other children. His son Thomas *"got no share of his money"!*

Harriet was a music teacher and the high ceilings of number seven rang with melody and the occasional discord. Harriet gave the house to her sisters Edith and Ellen who conveyed it to Thomas William Bussell on 29 May 1952.

During the war years the single storey extension, which opened unto the garden and Hibernia Street, became Redburn Café. It was patronised by military personnel from the Palace Barracks and by the teenagers of the town.

At that time temporary lodging accommodation was at a premium in Holywood. The tall house had a dozen rooms available to paying guests. Number seven was much in demand by those coming up from the country to help the war effort!

The Bussell family lived in the house for the next half century and contributed greatly to the social and commercial life of the town. For many years Councillor William Bussell enthusiastically represented Holywood on the North Down Borough Council.

The landmark property was demolished in 2002 and the vacant site acquired by Fold Housing Association.

LI RICHMOND LODGE (C.1800) A.P.D.L. KNOCKNAGONEY HOUSING ESTATE
BELFAST ROAD BT9 1SL

In his Statistical Memoir for the first Ordnance Survey (1834) Lieutenant G.F.W. Bordes describes Richmond Lodge as one of the gentlemen's scats studding the shore of Belfast Lough, all of which were ornamented with gardens and plantations.

Today the car park and pathways leading into the valley of Knocknagoney Linear Park mark the grand entrance and carriage avenue which led up to Richmond in its heyday. Originally, the gates were some hundred yards nearer the historic Ballymaghan Motte. They were guarded by a pretty little "ink-pot" lodge, rather like those of Ballymenoch House. The back gates opened unto Knocknagoney Road and here John Dunville built a second gate lodge (c. 1858). The lodge illustrated with this article was built (c. 1875) by John Kennedy. He acquired Richmond from the Dunville Family, refurbished the house and realigned the avenue.

My pencil sketch shows the house as I knew it in my teenage days. An engraving by E.K. Proctor (1832) shows the house before the Kennedy restoration, which replaced the small porch with the fine ten pillared colonnade. Perhaps at this time, the elegantly disguised water tower was erected in the court yard, rather like the Lanyon tower situated in the yard at Dundarave, Bushmills. Probably the house was built by the McCance family at the end of the eighteenth century. Like the neighbouring "big houses" it was built on the elevation of the raised beach which skirts the lough. The parkland extended to the shoreline and made provision for the Belfast and County Down Railway line in 1848 and the road works which transformed transportation between Holywood and Belfast in 1836. The Holywood Rose grew in profusion along the seaboard; we read its story when we visited Clifton House (Q.V.).

Like other entrepreneurs of those days, David McCance accumulated rent income from his properties. Francis Turnly (1766-1845) returned home from China about 1800 with a multi-million fortune accrued from three decades work as an East India merchant prince. He built various properties, became landlord of Cushendall and was related to the Batt Family of Purdysburn and John Turnly of Rockport. (Q.V.)

Francis Turnly planted 9,810 trees to "beautify the Richmond Estate which he rented about the year 1801 for £190 per annum. Many of the specimen trees can be seen in Proctor's engraving of the estate.

In his Antrim Coast property Francis Turnly built a fine schoolhouse (1820) and the beautiful Drumnasole House (c. 1819). The Antrim mansion is five bays wide and five deep, it has a dome over the stairwell and an unusual bell turret. The Parliamentary Gazetteer (1845) described it, *"a splendid mansion on a most romantic site"*. In Cushendall, Turnly built a tower *"as a place of confinement for idlers and rioters"*. (1809). It is 20 feet square, 40 feet high with projecting windows and battlements. James Boyle (Ordnance Survey Memoir 1835) recorded *"it is said to have been built after the model of some Chinese Tower"*.

When Francis Turnly died in 1845, David McCance discovered that the roof of the Richmond property was *"letting in the rain"* although John Turnly claimed that his father had

Gate Lodge

employed masons to repair the leaks!

The next occupant was John Dunville Esq. (1786-1851). Dunville advanced from a little apprentice boy in Napier's Distillery on Bank Street to owner of the company, which he re-formed under his own name The Royal Irish Distillery became one of the largest in the world, John became one of Belfast's leading citizen, wealthy and generous. He married Mary Grimshaw (1789-1865) and moved from the city into the country in 1845 to enjoy the salubrious setting of Richmond Lodge. Robert Grimshaw Dunville was born at Richmond in 1838 and removed a mile along the Old Holywood Road to build Redburn (Q.V.) in 1866. Other fortunate families occupied Richmond Lodge during those years when heating was affordable and staff available!

Sir Charles Brett recalls memories of his grandparents' sojourn at Richmond. *"In coronation year, my grandmother held a party during which the dining room table was covered with various regiments of British toy soldiers in procession. These were divided up amongst her grandchildren at the conclusion of the party".*

The estate with the specimen trees which Francis Turnly had planted in 1805, was acquired by Belfast Parks. The Big House was demolished to provide building sites for Knocknagoney Estate; although Richmond Nursery, in the old kitchen gardens, managed to remain in business for some years.

Richard Lodge held a special place in our heritage and was home to families which shaped our history. Its demolition added another tragedy to the long litany of forgotten Holywood houses.

Richmond Lodge

LII RIVERSTON HOUSE A.P.D.L. 66 CHURCH ROAD BT18 9BU

NURSERY SCHOOL AND TELEPHONE EXCHANGE

This handsome mansion (c.1858) replaced the watermill which gave its name to Mill Street, later called Church Street and then Church Road. The house took its name from the Ballykeel River of which the culverted water course was carried under the pleasure gardens. With the demolition of the mill went the removal of a row of eighteenth century cottages. At the same time Mrs Connor's coach house disappeared, it was used as a Mass-House before St. Patrick's Church was built on Church View in 1829. Today the Nursery School covers the lower part of Riverston's gardens and the telephone exchange occupies the upper options.

Early maps indicate a common driveway with Mill Moat (Q.V.). Both houses shared a profusion of garden paths and entrances unto both Church and Victoria Roads. Formerly the grounds ran down to Victoria Place, the terrace at the foot of Victoria Road which re-named Ballykeel Road to honour the popular Queen. On the west side of the grounds, numbers 56 to 62 Church Road have been built up to the former convex quadrant gates of the big house. The Holywood Abattoir, built about 1860, was within the property, it was demolished by the Housing Executive in 1982. When we were children, my brother and I were entranced by the circular elevated fish pond with its tall fountain, situated between the Motte and the long flight of steps which led to the wide double front doors of Riverston House.

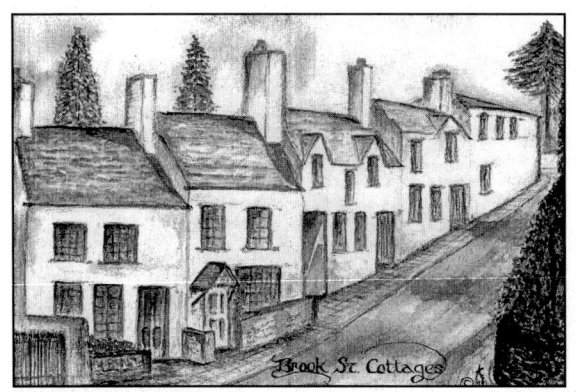

Riverston was built on the Brook Street boundary of the property to avoid disturbing the Anglo-Norman Motte. Rev. James O'Laverty claimed the cone shaped hill was the funereal mound of a local chief. Certainly Holywood was the government headquarters of John de Saukvill when Henry III confirmed his possession of Holywood in 1217, also it was a lodging for King John, when he visited Holywood on July 29, 1210.

In 1819 Rev. W.A. Holmes recorded *"To the south of the Church there is an artificial mound, 40 feet in diameter at top and 180 feet at base. It hangs over a burn and at that side is 50 feet in height. Two thirds of the base are surrounded by a deep fosse. The sides are planted with forest trees and overgrown with tangled bushes"*.

Writing in 1850, when J.B. Kennedy, a solicitor, was living in the Moat House, Surgeon T. Kelly records *"At the north-eastern extremity of the town an ancient rath is situated, now enclosed in a garden. Although it is considerably defaced by the hand of modern improvement, is still shows itself to be a relic of "Destiny obscure". These moulds seem to have been caused or altered for military purposes, at what age or by what people it is difficult to say. Though usually ascribed to the Danes, they are almost certainty the work of aboriginal tribes. The presence of burnt bones and funeral urns attest them to have been the scenes of the exploits of Irish Warriors. However, coins and other traces of the Danes are equally strong evidence of their occupation by that people"*.

Today the only portion of Riverston which remains is number 2 Brook Street; which was part of the service wing before the house was demolished in 1958.

In its earlier history Riverston House was the family home of the Browne family. Messrs Browne, Browne, Reid and Company were prosperous woollen merchants of Waring Street in Belfast. The best known residents were the Hughes family, Bernard Hughes Ltd. Model Bakery Springfield Road. Bernard Hughes Esq., had risen from obscurity in Armagh to the rank of Ireland's leading master baker. The family had lived on the Marine Parade before removing to College Square in Belfast. However, he always favoured Holywood and even brought his employees on holiday excursions to enjoy our sandy bathing beaches. When Bernard Hughes retired in 1868, he came back to live in Holywood until his death in 1878. He contributed generously to the building of St. Colmcilles Church (1874). The third window in the nave was inscribed *"Bernard Hughes, died 1878 aged 69 years and his wife Jane Hughes died 1847 aged 44 years"*.

One of the best loved clerics in the Province grew up at Riverston. In the 1920's the Murphy family were in residence; sons Hugh and Simon with the other boys about the town, enjoyed the private adventure playground with its ancient motte which surrounded the Murphy home. Father Hugh Murphy, later a naval chaplain, did much to bring peace to the troubled times of the 1970's.

After the Town Hall was destroyed by fire in 1940, the Urban District Council acquired temporary premises in the High Street and at Riverston House. Then the rafters rang with the laughter of many clubs and organisations. In 1947 the nursery school found its first home in Riverston and removed to a purposed built school on the lower part of the garden after the house was demolished in 1960. The site was used for the fourth location of Holywood Telephone Exchange which had removed from High Street to Mill Moat grounds in the 1930's.

To complete the Riverston story I should include a few words on Mill Moat House and the extant mill workers cottages on Victoria Road and Brook Street.

In my childhood days the house was known as the Moat and inhabited by Miss Burke of the Holywood post office. A moat is a wide water-filled ditch around a castle or fort. A motte is a twelfth century mound on which the Anglo-Normans erected a fortified courtyard, surrounding a wooden castle. Perhaps the Ballykeel River did provide water for a moat to surround the Holywood Motte. Mill Moat House may have been the residence of the owner of the mill in the grounds, which was demolished some time after 1834.

Mill Moat was refurbished in 1820, it became the home of the Read family in 1862. Robert and David Read founded *"Belfast Morning News"* in 1858, which became *"Irish News"* – that Belfast journal meticulous in the veracity of news reports. The Read family were generous benefactors to St. Colmcilles Church. The chancel arch carried Robert's name, windows commemorated David, his wife Catherine and their son Patrick. The font was inscribed to the Read family.

We are fortunate that this fine eighteenth century house is preserved in pristine condition by Dr. W. Stewart. The adjacent mill-workers cottages are extant. They were condemned by the Urban District Council. Fortunately the cottages have been faithfully restored by David Nimmons Esq., of Victoria House.

Mill Moat

Riverston House

Holywood Abattoir

LIII ROCKPORT HOUSE (C.1810) P.D.L. 15 ROCKPORT ROAD BT18 ODE
ROCKPORT SCHOOL

The earliest picture of Rockport House shows a five bay mansion with pillared portico. Two fashionably dressed gentlemen are observing the view over Belfast Lough. The picture shows five cottages scattered over the present campus of Glencraig Camphill Community (c.1832).

Rockport House was built in the early years of the nineteenth century by John Turnly Esq. J.P. (1764-1841). The Turnlys had another property in the Holywood area – Richmond Lodge on the Belfast Road (Q.V.). The family was well known on the Antrim Coast where Drumnasole, near Carnlough (c. 1819) was another Turnly Mansion. Their considerable wealth came from the Brewing Industry and overseas trade in the East India Company. John Turnly lived in Rockport until his death in 1841; he is memorialised in Holywood Parish Church as *"unostentatious and retiring, who lived a useful and happy life"*.

In 1820 Mrs Turnly established a school for local children at the gates of the mansion house. Over the following 182 years it has grown into one of our most prestigious primary schools – Glencraig.

Rev. W.A. Holmes (1819) records *"Rockport is modern, built by its present proprietor – John Turnly Esq. Its situation is close to the lough and near a small harbour from which it derives its name. It is nearly seven miles from Belfast, north side"*.

Lieutenant G.F.W. Bordes (1834) records Rockport as *"one of the gentlemens seats with which the shore of Belfast Lough is studded, all of which are ornamented with gardens and plantations"*.

By 1850 Surgeon Kelly merely indicates Rockport House *"as one of the commodious summer residences at Craigavad and Rockport"*.

The Turnly family remained in residence until the late 1850's, after which several owners occupied the property until 1906 when Geoffrey Bing Esq., M.A. acquired it as a campus for a private preparatory school. For almost a century Rockport School has been the leading independent school in the Province, its history is outlined in *"Holywood Then and Now"*.

At some time in its long history the house pictured in E K Proctor's engraving (1832) was considerably refurbished.

The neo-classical five bay, quoined mansion has a portico with columns and high moulded cornice complementing the extended eaves and modillion brackets which surround the hipped roof. String courses connect square pane windows with bracketed cills and extensive surrounding ornamentation.

Today the mansion with educational additions and athletic grounds are meticulously maintained; this local benison accrues from Geoffrey Bing's fortunate choice for the campus of his school in 1906.

LIV SEAPARK COTTAGE (C. 1820) A.P.D.L. SEAPARK ROAD, BT18 0DA

Originally Seapark was a small farm by the shores of Belfast Lough, on the east side of Holywood. As the town developed and fast public transport became available, the farm became valuable building ground for those who wished to live by the sea.

The extension of the Railway Line to Bangor divided the farm from the main road to Belfast. A tall sandstone arch provided entry to the farm, its use carefully guarded by gates. Marino Station (1865) provided easy access to the city. A *"Cinder Path"* ran down from the station, beside the railway line.

A second arch accommodated the right-of-way from the main road to the neighbouring farm "Marino Cottage". Presumably the Ballymenoch burn divided the two agricultural properties.

The first entrepreneurial development was Seapark Terrace, six tall town houses overlooking the lough shore. Locally, the houses were called the *"Windows' Terrace"* as several of the occupants had been married to deceased master mariners. In the early years of the twentieth century the land in front of the terrace was filled with an early housing estate – Seapark Avenue and Seapark Road – some twenty semi-detached houses.

About the same time, five or six villas were built on Ballymenoch Park (BT18 0LP). Soon others were added, one of the most attractive, *"Daisy Bank"*, was the residence of David Bell Esq., Holywood's efficient town clerk for thirty seven years. Formerly, the lane joining Seapark Road with Ballymenoch Park, commenced closer to the railway arch, affording space for an excellent hockey pitch. The Holywood Urban District Council developed the area into a recreation ground. Excavations for the proposed Holywood swimming pool can be seen at the car park. Half a century later the town still awaits that aquatic facility!

Thus it was in the latter years of the nineteenth century that the property ceased to be a farm cottage. The building was refurbished and greatly extended, although the original cottage could be discerned in the centre of the redesigned house. Two low towers and a new wing were added. Part of the old farm offices became garages and stores with a pretty little oculus window inserted into the gable wall. Quoins, elaborate barge boards with hipknobs and a crested roof ridge added decoration to the refurbishment. Several walls carried battlements to give an *"Antique Effect"*.

The interior received similar personal attention from an amateur enthusiast. The extensive well-manicured gardens with an entrancing little Wendy House were protected by an extravagant single wooden gate.

The effect of refurbishment was very pleasing and completely original. The house was demolished in 1997 to make way for Seapark Court, with its six apartments and Seapark Mews with six houses.

LV SORRENTO (c. 1875) A.P.D.L. GLEN ROAD BT18 OHB

Sorrento was well named after the Mediterranean Island, as its many square and canted bay windows commanding seaviews, allowed the high ceilinged reception rooms to be filled with southern sunshine.

The house flaunted a tall square tower with flag staff, from which the union flag fluttered when the Ross family of Lisburn were in residence. Generally the family arrived in their second home for summer holidays spent with the yacht clubs and golf links of North Down.

The many angled roof was completely surrounded by a stone balustrade, as was the tower. Accommodation was provided on three floors. A pillared porch led into a spacious hall from which opened capacious drawing-room, dining room, sitting room and billiards room. The culinary suite was extensive. Ten bedrooms, servants quarters, bathrooms and a second floor veranda completed the domestic provisions.

The grounds extended over acres of pleasure gardens. A curving wooded driveway approached the house from Glen Road. The stable yard and a spacious conservatory with vinery added to this comfortable North Down holiday retreat.

Sorrento was advertised for public auction in the Avenue Hall, Garfield Street, Belfast on 28th May 1943. It was purchased by the owners of the neighbouring property, Ardavon. Sorrento was demolished and the gardens brought into the Ardavon grounds to allow extension of a unique collection of hybrid rhododendrons.

Part of the Sorrento campus was added to the Dalchoolin Estate when the Transport Museum was added to the Ulster Folk Museum.

LVI SPAFIELD (1832) P.D.L. SPAFIELD FOLD, HIGH STREET BT18 9HJ

Originally there were four dwellings in the exceptionally fine Georgian Terrace built in 1832 by Jonathan Cordukes (1802-1865) and called after the neighbouring mineral water springs.

Surgeon Kelly (1850) writes, *"In the immediate vicinity of the town there have been observed several Chalybeate Springs, one of which we lately visited, presented the appearance of being largely impregnated with the metallic oxide. It is situated in front of the Spafield Buildings, from which these houses take their name. We are of the opinion that it is a strong and excellent chalybeate and might be used with great benefit where such a tonic is indicated"*. (Chalybeate means containing iron salts).

The Cordukes family hailed from Yorkshire and settled in Belfast shortly after 1820, where they prospered in York Street as provision merchants. Jonathan Cordukes became a Belfast Town Councillor in 1842 and later a Holywood Town Commissioner. Like so many others, it seems the Cordukes moved out of Belfast to the healthy Holywood countryside. As their prosperity increased the family removed to the west end of the parish where Glen Ebor, (later called Hampton), was erected in 1865 on Glenmachan Road. The Corduke Memorial was erected on the north wall within the old priory Church and is extant.

The terrace was the best example of late Georgian architecture in Holywood. Its dark brick façade carried traditional squared glazing, minimal ornamentation, good door cases, quoins and gable ogee windows. Inside the houses the ceilings of the exceptionally large reception rooms were decoratively stuccoed in the usual Holywood manner.

The first residents of the fine twelve bay terrace saw the good results of the Holywood bank (C.1830) which joined the Kinnegar peninsula with the mainland. Originally the Spafield pleasure gardens descended to the river estuary.

At the same time the two houses at the western end of the terrace became a single residence, although it retained two back yards and the divisional arrangements were rather insecure!

These listed buildings were allowed to deteriorate and were demolished in 1979, for the erection of Spafield Fold. Unfortunately Spafield scored four firsts! It was the first traditional Holywood Terrace for which the town became famous; it was in the first group of listed buildings in the area; it was the first fine building to be needlessly demolished in the teeth of local opposition; it was the first listed building in Holywood to be granted permission for demolition after its destruction had occurred.

In the days when a succession of well known Holywood families enjoyed the Spafield ambience, a line of large stones protected the carefully tended lawns from traffic. Today salubrious Spafield is memorialised in Windsor Avenue by the white stones.

Spafield Terrace

LVII STANLEY HOUSE (C. 1858) A.P.D.L. 138 CHURCH ROAD BT18 9BZ

Stanley House allows a cursory glance into Holywood's alternative history! In 1810 wealthy Belfast shipowner George Langtry acquired the Fortwilliam Estate which ran between Antrim Road and Shore Road. In 1863 it was divided into large building sites for mansion houses. George Langtry's grandson Edward (1848-1897) passed time sailing his 25 meter yacht *"Red Gauntlet"*. In 1874 harbouring at St. Helier, he fell in love with *"The Jersey Lily"*, Emilie Charlotte Le Breton. Lillie's father, the Dean of Jersey, married the couple in Saint Saviour's Church on the Hill, 9 March 1874. Edward refused a place in the family shipping business, preferring to live on his private income accrued from Belfast ground rents (£3,800). The young Langtrys set up house in "Noirmont Manor" on Jersey. Soon money ran out, "Red Gauntlet" was sold and the marriage was on the rocks. They removed to London's Eaton Place, where Edward turned to alcohol in order to drown his sorrows. In 1877 H.R.H. Prince of Wales saw the portrait of Lillie by J.E. Millais in Christies Auction House – the rest is history! Edward remained loyal throughout the cuckolding. To keep him from learning the full truth, Lillie sent her husband to the U.S.A. with an annuity to keep him happy. In 1897 Edward Langtry was picked up as a drunken vagrant in Chester, England, and imprisoned. Lillie paid his debts and bought medical opinion to have him declared insane. He died in Chester County Asylum on 15 October 1897. It seems Edward's grandmother, Mrs George Langtry was resident in Stanley House at that time.

The original lease for Stanley House was dated 29 January 1858, granted by John Harrison to William Weatherall for 999 years at an annual rent of £12.00. It became Lot 72 in the sale of Holywood Ground Rents in December 1917. At that time the tenant was J.B. Johnston .

William Weatherall built Stanley House during the same year in which he obtained the lease, not for himself but as property speculation, which was quite usual in those days.

The first resident of the fine new house was Hugh Rea Esq., a merchant, who moved to Church Road from the High Street.

For many years the house was the happy family home of Sir John and Lady Margaret McDermott. The property became associated with Marmion Children's home. It was demolished in the 1980's – the acre site of Stanley House remains vacant, although one of the entrance gate pillars still stands on Church Road.

Originally the house was rectangular with four bays on the west entrance front. A cornice and blocking course emphasised the hipped roof and pilasters terminated this façade. At some time the ground floor first and second openings had been replaced by a highly ornamental tripartite window. The door case was refurbished at the same time.

The garden front, with panoramic views over Belfast Lough, had two bay windows with balustrades. Above each were double windows with heavily supported coping. The ground floor left hand bay window was replaced by a large semi-elliptical extension with balustrade and fully glazed garden door. The extension created a specially fine and unusual reception room.

LVIII ST. HELEN'S (1876) P.D.L. 155 HIGH STREET BT18 9LG

St. Helen's was the home of the Dunlop Family. Dr Archibald Dunlop (1834-1902) hailed from Derriaghy in Co. Antrim. He came to Holywood as a young medical practitioner about the year 1860, when Dr. John Gabbey was approaching middle age and possibly surgeon Thomas Kelly was still operating his medical hall on the High Street.

Dr. Dunlop became a town commissioner and later a town councillor, also a Justice of the Peace, the town's medical officer, a governor of the Sullivan schools, a member of the select vestry and the people's church warden. The 'Good Samaritan' window in the north aisle of the Church of St. Philip and St. James was erected in memory of the good doctor. Dr. S.H. Dunlop, a younger son, was a select vestryman from 1892 to 1901.

The elder son, Captain George Malcolm Dunlop of the Royal Dublin Fusiliers was killed at the Dardanelles in the landing on Gallipoli Peninsula (April 1915). He was the first of many Holywood soldiers massacred in the Great War. Appropriately, his mother unveiled the Holywood war memorial on Saturday 28 January 1922.

The Dunlop Memorial was erected by public subscription in 1903 on Church-Road (Number 43 BT18 9BU). It was a home for the Holywood Nursing Society and served the community until 1956, eight years after the National Health Service came into being. At that time the house became the private home of the Muchison family. Mrs Muchison's father, James Hanna Esq designed the building in 1903. He was the well-known architect whose expertise is seen in many Holywood Houses. In 1984 the property was acquired by the Abbeyfield Society. The building was sympathetically enlarged by architect Neville M. Wilson. Today it provides a service dear to the heart of Dr. Archibald Dunlop.

St. Helen's is a square mansion in the Italianate style containing two main storeys with attic and basement floors. It was built in 1876 unto the ancient raised beach. The entrance front displays a large pillared and balustraded portico, and bay windows with balconettes on either side. First storey tripartite windows with concave open pediments surmount the bay windows. On the garden façade, which overlooks the lough, a vast bow-fronted bay is carried up the full height of the house from basement to attic. On this front, the windows are similarly decorated with corbels and concave or angled pediments. The house has quoins and string courses to each storey.

The hipped roof carries extended eaves with extravagant rafter supports, which ingeniously accommodate the attic windows. The interior of the house boasts a fine central and staircase hall, which is open to the first storey; splendid stucco work and panelling complete the essay.

During the years of the Second World War the house was requisitioned for military transport personnel. A line of garages was thrown up in the front garden. Today the garages are a small shopping complex. After the war the big house was divided into apartments. The lower gardens were used to erect St. Helen's Court, which provided 18 residential units on the Holywood High Street.

LIX THE FIRS (1889) P.D.L. 160 HIGH S TREET BT18 9HT HEADQUARTERS OF THE COUNCIL FOR CATHOLIC MAINTAINED SCHOOLS

The Firs is one of the best examples in Holywood of the Arts and Crafts movement (see Abingdon). It was built in 1889 by the Payne family. Reuben Payne Esq., was a well known merchant tailor with an extremely prosperous business in Belfast.

The house was part of the convoluted Lot 111, on a lease dated 21 May 1888. C K Cordner, John Harrison and Charles A. Wilson designated the representatives of Reuben Payne as tenants in 1917. The lessor had right of entry to a local private reservoir and the nearby river. Only two houses could be built on the three and a half acre site – one fronting Belfast Road the other towards Downshire Hill. There was to be no exposure of clothes for drying or bleaching, no nuisances and no use of the river except for domestic purposes.

The Maguire Family came to live in The Firs in the early years of the twentieth century. When Miss Kitty Maguire died in 1943, the house was bequeathed to the Sisters of the Cross and Passion. The following year the Sisters opened "Mount St. Mary" a private school; it closed in 1946.

In 1948 Mount St. Mary became a hostel for young women. In 1953 the school was re-opened, flourished and reluctantly closed in 1971. The sisters continued to provide valuable service to the Holywood community.

The small private school was replaced with a Grammar School for girls under the tutelage of the Sisters of the Sacred Heart of Mary. In 1985 the school was amalgamated with Our Lady's and St. Patrick's College, Knock. "The Firs" or "Mount St Mary" became the headquarters of the Council for Catholic Maintained Schools.

As with all Catholic Church property, the house is beautifully maintained. It was built in red brick and is characterised by its multitude of gables. A great protruding bay window catches the eye as one approaches the house over a delightful little balustraded bridge. The window cases carry curved heads and half square pane casements. There are string courses and wide eaves. The whole effect provides the impression of a very fine villa residence.

In 1893 Reuben Payne built a gate lodge at the Belfast Road entrance, in the same style as the big house. It is single storey on a cruciform plan. The windows have the separated upper glazing pattern of the house. The roof is earthenware tiled. A vertically ribbed brick chimney stack completes the pleasant picture on Holywood's High Street.

LX THE VICARAGE (P.D.L. 93A and B CHURCH ROAD AND WINDSOR AVENUE BT18 9BY)

When Rev. William Anthony Holmes came to Holywood parish in August 1810 he found the Priory House was situated on the upper side of the road to Bangor, almost opposite his Church. He described it as *"a small farm and orchard of about ten acres, which appeared was given in exchange for the present glebe"*. He decided to build a new Glebe House within the thirteen acres of ecclesiastical land on Church Road. This was achieved partly at his own expense and partly from Parliamentary Grants.

The incumbent described his new home as *"very convenient being scarcely a quarter of a mile from the Church and village. It stands on an eminence south-east of Holywood and commands a beautiful prospect of the Belfast Lough and the adjacent country"*. Rev. W.A. Holmes was our first local historian; the town owes much to the information he collected for a statistical survey of the parish. The vicar's perception allowed early recognition of young Robert Sullivan's scholastic brilliance. It was thought his efforts that Dr. Sullivan received the chance to become one of Ireland's leading educationalists.

By 1867 half of the original glebe lands had been let as building sites to accommodate the growing town. Parts of the early nineteenth century Glebe House are extant. However, in 1872 local builder William Nimmick was commissioned to remove two wings, refurbish windows, replace fireplaces and modernise the exterior décor. At that time the town sewage system was extended along Church Road to the Vicarage. The entrance was opposite the gates to Marmion and the six acres of park lands were well-wooded and laid out with sequestered shubbery pathways. For Holywood folk, especially little boys like myself, visits to the Vicarage were a great treat. I remember a baptismal font from the Old Priory surmounted a rockery which divided the driveway at the front door. In 1850 Surgeon Thomas Kelly tells us *"The stone font of the ancient priory is yet in perfect existence and is in the possession of Mr Hugh Stewart of this town"*. In 1884 Rev. James O'Laverty recorded *"The old Holy-water stoop, a basin of white marble which was found in the graveyard, was presented to the new parish Church by Hugh Stewart Esq.* In 1819 Rev. W.A. Holmes described *"A large piece of freestone, a cube of about four feet which seems, by an excavation of the size of a bowl, to have been used as a font"*. I wonder where this second Holywood cuboid is today?

After the Second World War the Vicarage park lands were given over to the twenty eight units of Windsor Avenue private housing development. In 1950 Rev. Canon Eric Barber removed his family to 156 High Street. Fortunately, the historic old house was saved from demolition. It was divided into two dwellings and is carefully preserved for posterity as private property.

The best known resident of Holywood Vicarage was Rev. John Baptist Crozier (1853-1920). He became Vicar of Holywood in June 1880 and departed in November 1897 when he became Bishop of Ossory, Ferns and Leighlin. In 1907 he was translated to the Diocese of Down, Connor And Dromore. Four years later he was elected Archbishop of Armagh, Primate of all Ireland. We are fortunate that the grand old house which illustrates much of Heritage Holywood has survived into the twenty first century.

LX1 WILLESDEN (P.D.L. 75 CHURCH ROAD) BT18 9BX

Willesden was built by John R. Neill Esq. about the year 1860, as a family home. The site at the corner of Church and Demesne Roads had been part of the Glebe. In 1868 a Report of the House of Lords recorded the building of Willesden and Woodville on church land. They commanded a fine view over the lough, before the parish church was enlarged in 1869. At that time the lane which ran along the south boundary of the site continued into Lemonfield and the Shepherd's Path. The present day line of Demesne Road did not materialise until the 1870's.

John R Neill was a partner in Neill Brothers, celebrated chronometer, watch and clock makers, gold and silversmiths, diamond merchants and opticians. The firm was established in Donegall Place about 1802, by 1886 it received a special appointment to the Prince of Wales under the name Sharman D. Neill. In 1900 the family removed the Ardmoyle, built at Cultra in the Arts and Crafts style

Williesden welcomed another family of wealthy merchant princes – the Finlays of Victoria Square, Belfast. Alexander Finlay's soap, candle and glycerin works was founded in 1788; it boasted one of the deepest wells and the tallest chimneys in Belfast City. Archibald Finlay was the last member of the family to live at Willesden. He was a kindly old gentleman with a pocket full of sweets for the children he loved to meet about the town. A talented scientist, he was intrigued by intricate mathematical problems. Finlay commissioned erection of a Mourne granite cuboid on the east lawn of Willesden The cuboid illustrates the recurring proportions of classical art and architecture. Constant ratio of dimension are recorded on the south face of the stone – $L/W = W/D = D^1/L$. The North face carries the ever resultant $2^1/_3$. J.J. Tohill in his essay *"Search of the Extraordinary"* claims a bar of Finlay's soap was an exact miniature in the proportions of the unique stone. Today the Holywood cuboid is the centrepiece of a garden in Church Avenue.

Willesden was re-organised and sympathetically enlarged into a first class nursing home. The building was demolished in 1999 and the site prepared for an apartment building.

Willesden

LX11 WOODVILLE (C.1860) 1 AND 3 DEMESNE ROAD BT18 9DQ

The Ordnance Survey of 1895 (revised 1938) records 1 and 3 Demesne Road under the name Woodville. The semi-detached houses were built on the former Glebe lands of the established Church of Ireland. Over the years many well-known Holywood families have enjoyed the comfortable life-style which the commodious houses presented, of which the McCammons were outstanding. Several of the Woodville families contributed greatly to the community and social life of the town.

For a short time in the twentieth century the houses were united to accommodate the Holywood Bible College. As with the neighbouring properties, the building was erected on the highest point of the site, to afford the best view over the town to the lough and the blue hills of Antrim.

The houses were built in the elaborate Victorian style of the nineteenth century, which characterised Holywood fashion of the day. Woodside had many gables of differing heights and many irregular bays. The architect successfully united square, semi-circular and segmental openings with tripartite, double and single windows. Canted bays, cornices, drip stones and elaborate quoins completed the picture – beautiful to behold, difficult to build and hard to maintain.

In August 2002 the houses were demolished while an emergency listing order was being sought from the Department of the Environment and the North Down Borough Council. Thus the erosion of our environmental heritage continues into the new millennium. I shall comment on the subject in the final essay.

An outstanding feature of Victorian Holywood Heritage is the group of large semi-detached houses which were erected by the business and professional families who chose the maypole sea-side town for permanent residence. Here I include examples of the grand semi-detached houses which contribute uniquely to Holywood Heritage. (D) = Demolished (A) = Converted into Apartments.

Alexandra Park	5 & 7 (Oakleigh & Ashleigh)
Bangor Road	1 & 3 (Churchfield) 9 & 11 (Ballykeel); 13 & 15 (Martello & Clifden); 102 & 104 (Lynwood) (A); 101 & 103 (Redholme & Craigmoyle); 162 & 164 (Glenview)
Church View	Churchill (D)
Church Road	112 & 114 (Riverside Terrace) 116 – 118 (Woodview); 120 & 122 (Innisfallen); Plas Merdyn.
Circular Rd West	Craig Royston and Cherrydeane.
Croft Road	13 & 15 (Hillcroft & Woodburn) 22 & 24 (Brook Croft)
Demesne Road	1 & 3 (Woodside) (D); 5 & 7 (Kilmore)
Downshire Rd	117 (Fernbank) Three Houses
High Street	Victoria Terrace; 152 & 154 (Ardeen & Laurel Lodge); 156 & 158 (Benthorpe & The Vicarage)
Kinnegar Road	22 & 24 (St Leonards)
Seafront Road	Clanbrassil Villas (D)
Tudor Park	1 & 2; 3 & 4; 5 & 6 (Three of the finest semi-detached houses in Holywood).
Victoria Road	22 & 24 (Hillbrook); 33 & 35 (Millbank & Victoria House); 61 & 63 (Glenside Place); 65 & 67; 85 & 87 (Claremont) 93 & 95 (Burnleigh & Crofton).

LXIII. EXAMPLES OF HOLYWOOD GATE PIERS

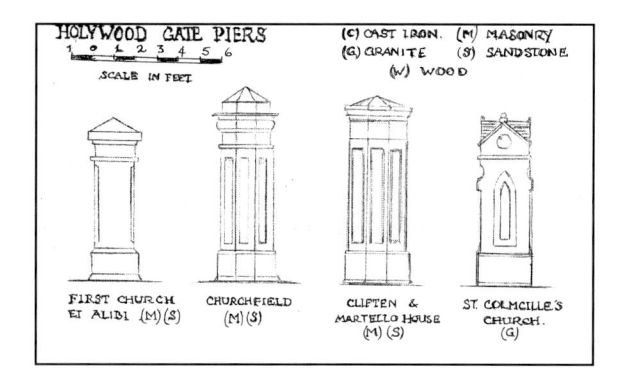

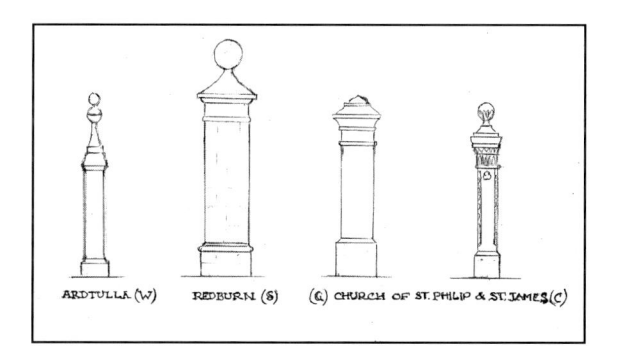

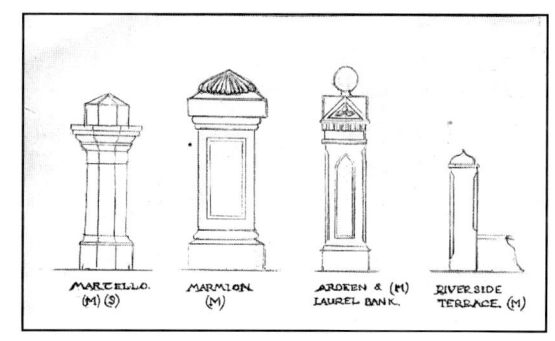

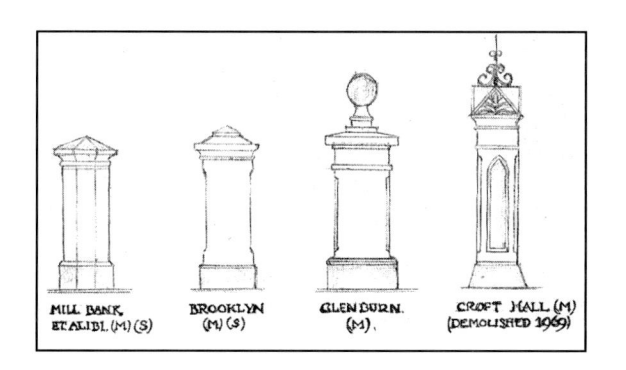

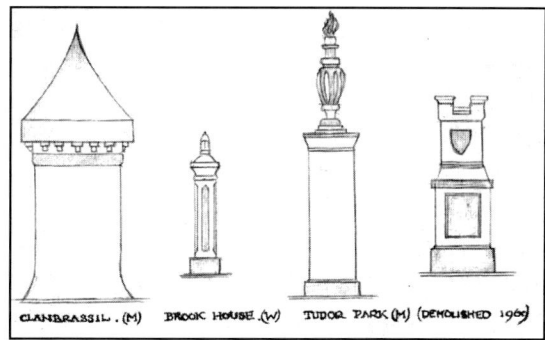

LX1V FINAL COMMENTS

I conclude the study of the forgotten houses of Holywood with a few comments on the demolition of our nineteenth century heritage mansions. We should endeavour to discover a method to preserve the considerable number of extant houses. The group of some twenty houses and two spectacular terraces in High Holywood is unique, because of their proximity to one and other. Other important groups are at Cultra and Craigavad. None can ever be replaced after demolition.

Melioration may be achieved by the following and other suggestions.

1. Cost of refurbishment of heritage properties is subject to value added tax. Demolition of the property and new build on the site is exempt from V.A.T. Abolition of V.A.T. on maintenance of heritage property is recommended.
2. Upkeep cost of heritage houses with extensive pleasure gardens is prohibitve in the twenty first century. The fact that such properties provide a valuable free amenity to the community should be taken into consideration when the net annual valuation is calculated.
3. Many older residents in life-long family homes do not use the local facilities for which they pay heavily in over rated properties. A flat rate charge levied on all individuals to whom the services of the District Councils are available would be a fairer method of local rates collection; or a reduction for senior citizens who continue to live in their heritage houses.
4. Promotion of the three groups of heritage houses in the Holywood area as a unique tourist attraction would attract special grants, enhance local economy and engender finance for maintenance and development of the heritage houses.

Example of The Natchez Experiment

In the 1930's Natchez, on the river Mississippi, USA was a town of fine old plantation mansions, mouldering away as a result of the Depression years. Banks were foreclosing on double mortgage debts, residents had reached the limit of endurance. The grand old heritage houses were being demolished by their owners to keep body and soul together. Today Natchez is a world heritage show place, attracting tens of thousands of enthusiastic visitors every year!

In 1931 the Mississippi State Federation of Garden Clubs arranged its annual general meeting in Natchez. On the eve of the meeting day the area suffered one of those bitter blighting freezes, of which we in Ireland know nothing.

There were no gardens worth putting on show. What was to be done? The local committee turned to their houses as show places, rather than their wilted gardens! The statewide visitors were pleasantly surprised by the enforced change of programme.

The following spring a "Pilgrimage of Natchez Mansions" was organised. Participating owners formed a business association. They hoped that admission charges would restore the beauty of their old residences and pay off the piles of debt.

The rest is history. Tourists love to see the inside of other people's homes and hear the stories of resident families. Today the Natchez Pilgrimage is one of the most brilliant stars in the U.S.A Tourist Programme. Annually it brings millions of dollars into the local economy and gives pleasure to thousands of tourists from all over the world. Owners no longer demolish their valuable properties. Their houses are the geese which lay golden eggs to maintain traditional lifestyles. We could emulate the Natchez experience in Holywood. For "starters" three of the Natchez houses have North Down names – "Belfast", "Richmond" and "Dunleith"!

The heritage trail and the thirteen hundred years recorded history of our town could be the answer to the demolition problem.

Con Auld

Fecit

2003

13 & 15 Bangor Road

9 & 11 Bangor Road

LXV GLOSSARY

(F) French; (L) Latin or Medieval Latin; (G) Greek: (I) Italian; (P) Plural;

(O.E.) Old English;   (O.F.) Old French.

Architrave	Lowest division of entablature or moulded frame around door or window. (I) Main beam, trave, (L) stem trab).
Archivolt	A decorative moulding on the face of an arch. The underside of an arch. (L.) Arcus – Arch plus Volta – a vault.
Ashlar	Masonry or squared stones in regular courses. (L.) Axicellus, - a plank
Attic	Upper storey above main cornice. Rooms within a roof (L.) Atticus
Arris	Sharp edge made by two surfaces meeting (L.) Arista – sharp edge.
Baluster	Small pillar or column supporting handrail or coping. (P) Balustrade (G.) Balaustion (shape of) pomegranate flower.
Balconette	As Balustrade.
Barge Board	Ornamental Board along gable end of roof (L.) Bargus – A Gallows.
Barge Course	Overhang of roof at gable or top.
Battlements	A defensive or decorative parapet with indentations (F.) Bateiller to fortify.
Bays	Special area or compartment into which roof, walls etc. of a building is divided. (F.) Bayer – to gape or stand open.
Bay Window	A Projecting Window.
Bracket	Projecting support for a weight – also modillion, console and ancone.
Campanile	A free standing bell tower (I.) Campana – a Bell.
Canted Bay Window	Side windows of bay set at slope to straight centre window.

GLOSSARY

Casement	A wide hollow in a wall. A window which opens on hinges as distinct from a sash.
	(L. Capsa - a box.
Chamfer	A diagonal cutting off of an arris. (F.) Chanfrein, - a channel.
Coffer	A sunk panel in ceilings. (L.) Cophinus (G.) Kophinos – a basket.
Colonade	A range of columus (L) Columna.
Concave	Curved inward like the inner surface of a sphere (L) Concavus, - hollowed out.
Conical roof	Cone shaped roof on a tower. (G.) Konos - pine cone.
Convex	Outwardly curved like the exterior surface of a sphere. (L) convexus – valuted.
Coping	Capping or top covering of a wall (L.) Capa, - cloak or hood.
Corbel	A carved or moulded projecting stone supporting a weight. (L. Corvus – a raven i.e. beak-like profile.
Cornice	Upper portion of entablature or any crowning projection. (G.) Koronis – Copestone.
Coupled Chimney-Stack	Two diagonally or square set stacks on same plinth (L) Copula – a binder, cord, rope
Cresting	Ornamental roof ridge tiles. (L.) Crista – Tuft or plume.
Cusped	A pointed projection formed by the intersection of two arcs. (L.) Cuspis – the pointed end of anything.
Diagonal Set	(G.) Diagonios – from angle to angle.
	Set in an oblique or slanting line
Door Case	Moulded surround to a door. (O.E.) Duru or dor -gate.

GLOSSARY

Dormer	A window in a sloping roof (F.) Dormir to sleep i.e. usually found in bedrooms.
Drip Stone	Projecting moulding over door or window to throw off rain, hood-moulding (O.E.) Dryppan – to drop.
Eaves	Lower part of roof projecting beyond face of wall (O.E.) Efes – over.
Entablature	Architrave, frieze and cornice supported by colonade or wall, (I.) Intavolatura – Boarding.
Façade	Face or elevation of a building (I). Facciata – Face.
Facia	Vertical face of projection around roof (L.) Facies – Face. Facia board in timber often ornamented.
Fanlight	Fan shaped window above a door (L). vanus, a winnower's fan now sometimes square.
Finial	Upper portion of pinnacle (L) Finis – end Any top decoration.
Frieze	Middle division of entablature (L.) Phrygium (opus) i.e. Phrygians were noted for craftmanship.
Gable	Triangular portion of wall enclosed by a sloping roof (O.F).Gafl.
Hipknob	Perpendicular pendant and pointed finial at end of gabled roof. (O.E.) Hype and (G.) Knobbe – Bud.
Hipped or Hip Roof	Enclosed by a sloping roof ends as well as sides (O.E.) Hype-a-hip
Jambs	Sides of doors, windows and fireplaces (O.F.) Jambe – Leg.
Keystone	Central stone of semicircular arch. (O.E.) Caeg.
Label Moulding	Rectangular dripstone (O.F). A ribbon.
Lancet Arch.	Sharp pointed arch. (L.) Lancea – a light spear.
Lintel	Horizontal timber or stone which spans an opening and supports a weight. (L.) Limitaris – Boundary.
Lozenge	A diamond shaped device or ornament. (O.F.) Losenge – a small square cake.
Modillions	Brackets

GLOSSARY

Mouldings	Countours given to projecting members (L.) Modulari – to be measured.
Mullions	Vertical members dividing windows into different numbers of lights (O.E). Moinel – Middle Part.
Newel	Post into which a handrail is framed (F.) Novel – a knob).
Octyhedral Roof	Eight sided roof on tower. (L.) Octo. (G.) Okto – Eight.
Oculus	A small circular opening or window (L.) Oculus – Eye.
Ogee	Moulding made up of convex and concave curves.
Oriel	Window corbelled out from face of a wall (O.F. oriol-poarch).
Panel	A sunk or raised compartment in walls, ceilings, doors etc. (O.F.) Pan – a piece of cloth.
Parapet	Low wall above roof gutter (L.) Parare – to guard plus pectus – brest. A blocking course.
Pediment	A triangular wall above the entablature, perhaps from (E.) Pyramid (L.) Pyramis (G.) Puramis.
Pilaster	A feature in pillar shape attached to a wall and projecting one sixth of its breadth. (L.) Pilastrum or Pila a Pillar.
Plinth	Square base of column; projecting base of a building (G.) Plinthos – tile, building stone.
Portico	Space forming an entrance with roof supported by columns. (L). Porticus from Porta – A Gate.
Purlin	Horizontal roof beam resting on principal rafters.
Quarry Tile	Quarter Square Stone Tile (L.) Quadrum – Square and (O.F.) Quarre – Square Cut Stone.
Quoin	Corner Stones at angles of buildings (F.) Coin – An Angle.
Ridge	Apex of Sloping roof (O.E. Hrycg – Back or spine).
Rustication	Stonework with rough ended surfaces (L.) Rusticus from rus – country).
Soffit	Underside or ceiling of any member (L.) Suffixus – fixed under.

GLOSSARY

Spandrel	Triangular space enclosed by curve or arch. (L.) Expandere – to spread out.
Storey	Space between two floors (L.) Historia, perhaps because historic scenes were painted on walls.
String Course	Moulding course running horizontally around the face of a building. (O.E.) Streng – stiff or strong.
Tripartite	Made up of three parts (L.) Tres – Three.
Under Panel	Panel set under a window.
Vermiculated Quoins	Decorated with wavy lines like the tracks of a worm. (L) Vermiculari – to be full of worms.
Vestibule	Ante-room to larger apartments (L.) Vestibulum.

LXVI INDEX

Abattoir	84	Burnleigh	12	Cultra House	41
Abbeyfield	90			Cultra Manor	41
Abingdon	11	Church Hill Manse	63		
Agricultural College	12	Clanbrassil Terrace	29	Dalcoolin	43
Alma Terrace	14	Clanbrassil Villas	30	Dalcoolin Gate Lodge	44
Alms Houses	15	Clifton	57		
Altona	16	Craigavad House	31	Easdale	45
Ardtullagh	17	Craigavad Gate Lodge (1)	32	Elton House	46
Ardville	19	Craigavad Gate Lodge (2)	48	Esplanade Cottage	47
Ashfield	21	Craigdarragh	33	Esporta	60
Bath Cottage	23	Craigdarragh Gate Lodge	32		
Ballymenoch House	25	Craigowen	48	Firs (The)	91
Ballymenoch Gatelodge (1)	25	Craigtara	34	Final Comments	96
Ballymenoch Gatelodge (2)	26	Croft Cottage	35		
Ballymenoch Cottages	26	Croft House	36	Gate Piers	95
Bangor Road No. 9 – 15	97	Crofton	12	Glenavon Manse	63
Beechcroft Manse	62	Crofton Hall	38	Glencraig	48
Bishop's Palace	21	Crofton Hall Gatelodge	38	Glencraig Gate Lodge	48
Brooklyn	27	Culloden	39	Glenside Manse	62
Brook Street Cottages	82	Culloden Gate Lodge	39	Glossary	98

INDEX

Golf House	46	Marine Hotel	65	Redburn Front Porch	78
Gray's Buildings	50	Marmion Lodge	66	Redburn Square No. 7	79
		Maryfield	68	Richmond Lodge	80
High Street No. 28	69	Maryfield Gate Lodge	69	Richmond Gate Lodge	80
Hillbrook	51	Mertoun Hall	58	Riverston House	82
Holywood House	52	Mill Moat House	83	Rockport House	85
Holywood House Gate Lodge	53			Seapark Cottage	86
Holywood Hill House	18	Oakley	70	Sorrento	87
House of Industry	54	Old Golf Club Pavillion	17	Spafield Terrace	88
Index	103	Old Palace Bar	75	Stanley House	89
Keeper's Cottage	18	Old Presbyterian Kirk	23	St. Helen's	90
Killips Court	56	O'Neill's Place	72	St. Valentine's	11
Knocknagoney House	60			Stewarts Place Cottages	24
Knocknagoney Gate Lodge	57	Patton's Lane	73		
Knocknagoney Cottage	58	Pebble Lodge	74	The Firs	91
Knocknagoney Farm	59			The Firs Gate Lodge	91
Knocknagoney Cottages	59			Vicarage	92
Lorne	61	Redburn House	76	Willesden	93
		Redburn Gate Lodge	77	Woodburn	37
		Redburn Cottages	78		
Marine Cottage	64	Redburn Belfast Gate Lodge	78	Woodville	94